MOTIVATED

by the

IMPOSSIBLE

D1300498

Edited by Nina Engen and Susan Brill
Cover page and layout design by Monika Clifton – VDesign, LLC
Graphic images by Monika Clifton and Trevor Shackleton
Cover and biography photos by Karissa Roe Photography

Published by CD Publishing – Seattle, WA
Printed by CreateSpace, An Amazon.com Company
Library of Congress Control Number: 2017904457

ISBN-13: 978-0-69286-375-6
ISBN-10: 0-69286-375-3

DEDICATED TO

EVERY BRAVE MAN OR WOMAN

who is motivated to look into the mirror of his or her own beautiful soul and find peaceful acceptance of who he or she has become, not based on perfection but on the relentless pursuit of recognizing the impossibilities of life as the ultimate invisible mentors.

JESUS,

the One and only, who knows my deepest secrets, my dreams and passions; whose love removes my shame, silences my fears, and gives me eternal life and peace.

CONTENTS

ENDORSEMENTS

Since she became a follower of Jesus Christ, Ceitci's entire life has been a continuum of faith, adventure, and personal growth. In her book *Motivated by the Impossible: Recognizing Your Invisible Mentors,* she creatively wraps events from her own experience with principles to motivate people to believe beyond the *possible.* This is a book for old and young alike, a challenge to new and seasoned faith, and ultimately a testimony to the faithfulness of God Himself to all who will trust Him completely.

LaDonna Osborn, D.Min.
President & CEO – *Osborn Ministries International*
Tulsa, Okla.

Ceitci's writing weaves together biblical insight, psychological understanding, and powerful stories in a beautiful tapestry of truth and inspiration. Each chapter invites the reader to engage in an interactive journey of discovery. Ceitci models courage and vulnerability as she generously allows us a front-row seat to what she learned from the invisible mentors in her life. We glean from the gift she offers, inspired toward fully becoming all that God has for us to be! I recommend this book to any person willing to be motivated by the impossible.

Beth Russell, M.A., LCPC, LPC, NCC
Executive Director – *Serenity Life Resource Center*
Kansas City, Mo.

As you read through Ceitci's book, purpose will be defined at the core of your being. The strength in each chapter will lift you above the external circumstances of life, and you will examine where you are and why you are there. Every chapter will snatch you from your present spiritual location and challenge you to go beyond what you considered was possible as you "embrace the impossibility." Ceitci has successfully orchestrated a verbal musical that will resound in your soul and cause your spirit to sing again. She has taken characters from the Bible and given them new life and relevance to our own journey as she also reveals her life experiences. This book will captivate you for hours. Absolutely refreshing!

Dave Dolan
Senior Pastor – *New Life Church*
Sullivan, Ill.

Many times, the difference between success and failure is perspective. In her book *Motivated by the Impossible,* Ceitci draws deep from the places of impossibility to motivate a current generation to arise to their purpose. Using her personal stories, she inspires the leader within the reader to see beyond the impossible to a life filled with joy and success. Allow this book to clean the lenses of your past and help you see the future that God has designed for you.

Luke Hodges
Lead Pastor – *Northstar Church*
Olympia, Wash.

When I think of my dear friend, the words *nothing is impossible* come to mind. I met Ceitci when we were both teenagers at Victory Bible College in Tulsa. She had just arrived to America with $100 in her pocket and 100 English words. Over the years, I have personally watched her tackle every challenge that life could throw at her with tenacity and unwavering faith that has been a constant source of inspiration for my own life. This book uncovers the untold stories of how she's done it, and it has launched me into a new revelation of how to take the adversities of life and turn them into a catalyst to fulfill the dreams inside my heart.

Christa Baca
Cofounder – *Go International*
Tulsa, Okla.

From the moment I met Ceitci, I have known her to be a woman after God's heart. It has been my privilege to walk with her as my "spiritual daughter" through many seasons of life. You will be very blessed reading her latest book, *Motivated by the Impossible.* In each of the chapters, you will savor unique stories from Ceitci's past used as a springboard to a life message. A surprise awaits at each conclusion where the reader can insert his or her unique life experience in an imagery exercise. Each chapter builds on the previous one, encouraging the reader to reach his or her destiny. Motivating and captivating, she challenges her readers to move forward in their journey.

Laurie Hobart
President – *Changing a Generation*
Seattle, Wash.

Motivated by the Impossible is a must read for anyone who values personal growth, embracing his or her greatest potential and the strength needed to live in such a way! Ceitci's insight in correlation with her personal stories brings the truth in this book to life! I found it completely inspiring and compelling to incorporate these insights daily. It's so far beyond a self-help book…it's transformative in the best way possible. I have been able to identify and strengthen many areas of my life as a result. My life is certainly enriched, and I believe that yours will be too.

Brey Noelle
Entertainer/Online Personality
Los Angeles, Calif.

The power of this book is that its author has lived out the keys, principles, and truths presented in it. Through her own life experiences, historical events, and biblical examples, Ceitci shows how obstacles, traumas, and even mistakes, can be seen and used as opportunities to learn, grow, and be transformed. Ceitci writes in very practical, real-life terms that are easy to relate to, grasp, and apprehend. Anyone who reads this book will come to a deeper understanding of transformation, the process of being conformed to the image of Jesus Christ.

Barry and Shawn Lenhardt
Lead Pastors – *International Life Center*
Portland, Oreg.

ACKNOWLEDGMENTS

I would like to express my sincere gratitude and appreciation to:

My wonderful father, Angel:

I am honored to be your daughter. Thank you for the beautiful memories we have created as a family over the years! It is because of you and Mom that I am able to write many of the principles in this book! You are and will always be my hero! I love you!

Beth Russell:

You are my best friend and my soul sister! Thank you for always speaking truth into my life, for believing in me and with me, for showing me how to be authentic, present, and fulfilled! I love you and I am so thankful to the Lord for bringing you into my life!

Pastor Bill Wilson:

Thank you for always believing in me and encouraging me to become all that God has created me to be! I am forever grateful for your friendship and for your life of dedication, sacrifice, and significance!

Bishop LaDonna Osborn:

You are my ultimate example of what it means to walk in true humility, to love as Christ has loved us, to speak with boldness and power, to be honest and true to God's calling! I love you and cherish our friendship!

Diane Tice:

Grateful to have met you and Lou at a time when I needed renewed hope and strength! Thank you to both of you for founding The Pacific Institute and creating a curriculum that has influenced the world and has served as a catalyst in my life and in the writing of this book.

Laurie Hobart:

Thank you for loving me as your own daughter and "adopting" me into your family—I am forever grateful! Your faith in God inspires me and encourages me to always remain close to Him! I love you!

Nina Engen and Susan Brill:

Your wonderful editing skills, dedication to the task, and professionalism were instrumental in making this book a reality. Thank you for believing in the message of this book and helping me present it in a clear and concise form, bringing the reader to a place of personal experience and insight!

Monika Clifton:

Thank you for creating the beautiful graphics and layouts within the pages of this book and for making my writings become alive, personalized and experiential for each reader! I love you and I am very thankful for your talent and friendship!

A special thank you to the following amazing people who journeyed with me during the writing and editing of this book—your encouragement and support helped me to bring this project into the world: Brey Noelle, Kelly Stark, Christa Baca, Pastors Luke and Jaimee Hodges, Pastors Dave and Debra Dolan, Pastors Barry and Shawn Lenhardt, and Shirley Martin Zumalt. Last but not least, a heartfelt thank you to Jeff Eadie—for enriching my life with your friendship and care, and to Betty Eadie, for your insightful wisdom and contribution in bringing hope and love to countless people around the world. I love you all!

Thank you to my family, my staff, partners of our nonprofit organization, and friends who are a part of my life. Though I can't mention all of your names on this page, your encouragement, support and prayers are greatly appreciated and will never be forgotten. Together we make our world a better place!

FOREWORD

As we journey through life, inevitably we will encounter trials and battles through which we must fight. People often pray that God will deliver them from the difficulties they face or that He will give them strength for the battle. They fear being bruised and battered in the fight. That is not how it works. A leader is not born in a day but in the fire—tried in the battle and proven in the tests of life. We don't get strength *for* a battle; we get strength *from* the battle. The only way to build resilience to withstand what is ahead is to press through the current impossibility, not go around it.

In today's world, we want success to come easily, without failure or setbacks. We are surrounded by people who quit before they give their efforts a chance to produce. But to be a champion who makes a difference in the world takes years of preparation. It takes not giving up in the midst of pain and difficulty but seeing beyond the present situation into God's possibilities and power. We need men and women who know how to fight and will not go home till the battle is won. We need people who have gone through the fire and survived as warriors.

This is Ceitci's story and the message she portrays in her book *Motivated by the Impossible.* I met her while she was still in her early twenties, and it has been my privilege over the years to watch her go through each of life's trials and come out on the other side with greater faith and deeper commitment to God and to the call on her life. The main reason this book is powerful and resonates with me is that Ceitci has lived every principle and revelation written in these pages. It's a message born from her darkest struggles, and it has the power to transform your life as a reader, to bring strength and courage for you to overcome any impossibility you may face.

Throughout my life, I have learned that it's not so much about a talent a person has, as much as it is about commitment. What will you do when you are stuck between a rock and a hard place? Will you give up, or will you stay committed to God—to your purpose, to the people entrusted to you, to the generations waiting to hear the message born within you from the battle? This is when you are tested! If you choose to be a person who chases after God, you will find yourself in situations that are not very pleasant. How you come through those circumstances depends on your reliability, your principles, your character, your consistency.

While you may never fight the battles Ceitci has had to fight, or go through the fires she's had to face, you can learn from her story and the principles shared in this book. They transcend culture and tradition. They are practical and insightful. You can learn how to see your current battles and impossibilities as *mentors*. You can choose to embrace them rather than reject them and to seize the moment of opportunity to help someone else, in spite of your own weakness. I have always believed that one person can make a difference, but your commitment and mine must be stronger than our emotions, and our vision must be more focused toward others than toward ourselves.

Motivated by the Impossible is a must read for everyone who desires to remain strong, resilient, and courageous in the midst of opposition and to live a life of servitude to others. It's for every man and every woman who wishes to use his or her voice in this world to bring forth God's truth and wisdom to this generation and to the generations to come! Get ready for a life-changing reading experience!

Bill Wilson, Ph.D.
Founder and Pastor, Metro World Child
www.metroworldchild.org

HOW TO READ THIS BOOK

In order to best understand and make the most of these principles, please begin with the introduction and read each chapter in sequence. Each one builds on insights from previous chapters. The progression is important to help you effectively apply the lessons to areas of your life.

Take time to think, write, and honestly answer the questions after each chapter.

May God guide you on this journey and open your eyes to the ways He desires to transform you in this season of your life.

Cheering you on to greatness!

❝ The only journey is the journey within."[1]

– RAINER MARIA RILKE

INTRODUCTION
THE JOURNEY AWAITS

The city of Seattle was dazzling. Light reflections painted the still waters of Puget Sound, and the view from Alki Beach, especially on a clear night like this, was breathtaking.

It revives you.

It inspires you.

It creates hunger in you for more:

to be more alive, to dream more freely, to believe more fearlessly.

Have you ever experienced being in a place where you realize from the moment you arrive that everything speaks of destiny, significance, and a worldwide impact on many lives? That was exactly where I was that night.

---

[1] BookLover, *Treasury of Motivational Quotes,* Kindle Edition.

As I stood by the library window of The Pacific Institute's corporate offices and gazed into the city skyline for literally hours, I knew this particular moment would never repeat itself. My heart became still and I tried to absorb into my innermost being as much of my surroundings as I possibly could.

Deep gratitude washed over me as I reflected on the transformation I had experienced in my life in just four short years since I first walked into this building and met Lou and Diane Tice, founders of the Institute.[2] Their spirit and vision were expressed in every picture, every piece of décor, and even in the individual construction of each floor. Appreciation gifts and plaques displayed from around the world spoke of the countless faces and lives touched because of these two people who had a noble cause.

The building itself held priceless memories. From hosting presidents, dignitaries, and influential businesspeople to elevating the dignity and self-esteem of teens and individuals who had lost their passion for life, it was a place of refuge as well as a training center and launching pad for dreamers and visionaries.

While I had been at this fifth-floor window looking at the Seattle skyline many times before, this particular night—December 5, 2014—was significantly different. In an instant, my thoughts flew back to the day, exactly twenty years earlier, when I stepped off the plane at JFK airport in New York from Sofia, Bulgaria. A shy, insecure teen, I arrived in America without family or friends, with just $100 in my wallet and a handful of English words.

Big dreams.

Even bigger fears…

And a lot of questions…

How could one who had lived under communist dictatorship, without identity or ability to choose, survive in this land of independence, individualism, aspiration, and endless opportunities?

As I reflected back, I realized that life had turned out so much better than what I had prayed and expected. Not because everything I wanted had come to pass in an instant. Not because it was easy. But because it was extremely hard!

And now I was here, surrounded by beautiful memories and history, completely at peace with my own thoughts, desires, and imperfections. Wow! That in itself was a miracle! Strengthened by the knowledge of the opportunities I had been given to

---

[2] This particular experience took place during my last visit to The Pacific Institute's building. Two years earlier, on April 1, 2012, Lou Tice passed away, and in 2015 the company sold the building and relocated.

observe and work with some incredible world leaders. No longer afraid of failing God or my family. Finally free to be fully myself.

I felt God whisper into my heart. "You are now equipped to write your book, *Motivated by the Impossible.*"

For many years I had carried the title hidden in my thoughts and prayers and envisioned the day I would write about the transformational principles one could use in changing the world. Little did I know that "motivated by the impossible" had nothing to do with changing the external world, but everything to do with the changes we implement inside our own selves—mind, body, and soul. The integration of who we are, freely expressed in what we do at all times and all places, can often be hard, even seemingly impossible. What we believe serves as the motivating factor to recognize our trials and impossibilities as the *invisible mentors* that challenge our perceptions and change our views—both inwardly and outwardly.

The word *journey,* according to Webster's Dictionary, is defined as "an act of traveling from one place to another." The journey of life reveals both our strengths and our weaknesses. It tries to expose our fears and can leave us in the ditch of shame, insecurity, and abandonment if we are not careful. Yet when we find the courage to live with authenticity backed with integrity, when we stop hiding behind the world's view of success, when we begin to fully understand our humanity and the need for complete dependence and surrender to God, then we are finally

> free from the distress of the screaming voices of the impossibilities.
> Free from the fear of being found out as fake.
> Free from people's opinions.
> Free from the false sense of external
> perfection while
> inwardly dying.
> Free to let people inside the
> "glass castle" of our heart,

where we give them permission to share in our quest for complete wholeness by no longer seeking their admiration. No longer intimidated by their perceived greatness, we finally release control of power and allow them to shine their own light, even in the path of our own alleys of life.

Problems, fears, and challenging circumstances are never something we choose, but their presence in our lives demands a certain response on our part. The way we view our past mistakes and our present or future impossibilities will determine the way we deal with them. They either define us or we define them. We have three choices: to ignore them, to fear them or to be motivated by them.

As we learn how to pay attention to the obstacles and begin to view life's challenges as one-on-one "boot-camp" with an invisible mentor standing next to us, we will emerge stronger, wiser, and more fearless.

This book will help you discover in a biblical, practical, and experiential way how to face your struggles without constantly taking a defensive approach, and how to rise above past disappointments without carrying them as a future regret or shame. It will give you the ability to view the broken pieces of life as a kaleidoscope that creates a beautiful picture of your journey on this earth. As you learn to spin your experiences to the correct focus and lighting, they become properly illuminated and serve as an encouragement to others who are motivated by the impossibility of finding themselves and their Creator.

I am here to simply tell you that you are qualified to overcome what seems impossible by first recognizing it as a mentor with a specific purpose. Embrace this journey of personal discovery. As you read each chapter, place the principles in the areas where your heart longs for the most liberty. May the analogies, teachings, and stories shared here serve to uncover the courage to not just pass through life's journey, but to overcome and release the captivity of your soul into the greatness of the potential God has placed in you.

The journey of discovery and freedom awaits you!

Your Fellow Sojourner,

Ceitci D.

Ceitci Demirkova

AN *INVISIBLE* MENTOR IS…

To best understand and glean strength, resilience, authenticity, and joy from the trials and impossibilities you face throughout your life, I would like to offer my description of an invisible mentor. What it is and how it influences us will help us better understand the premise of this book and the principles offered in it.

An *invisible mentor* is
    each impossibility,
        past or current,
            visible or invisible,
                sometimes created by our own choices
                    due to ignorance or arrogance,
                        at other times because of pride or naiveté,
perhaps dependent or independent of our decisions,
    yet, somehow present in our reality.

Its presence challenges our core beliefs, desires to undermine our values, exposes our weaknesses, silences our voices, and eliminates our dreams.
    It carries a specific voice. It has an undermining purpose.
        Sometimes it screams loudly through fear,
           regret, or shame…
              It tries to define us and imprison us to
                  surrender to a life of mere existence
                  and defeat.

We are faced with a choice,
    to either allow its existence to destroy us and
        define our future,
            or
to *recognize* it as an *invisible mentor* placed in our life to deepen our faith, overcome our fears, develop inward resilience and authenticity built through internal strength and character.

THE INVISIBLE MENTORS OF IMPOSSIBILITIES CAN BECOME OUR BEST FRIENDS, IF WE CHOOSE TO EMBRACE THEM AS SUCH.

DANCING ON HOT COALS

IT DRAWS A CROWD, BUT THE FIRE CAN DESTROY YOU

chapter

What we achieve inwardly will **change** outer reality."[1]

– PLUTARCH

THE WAIL of the Bulgarian goatskin bagpipe—the *gayda*—and the beat of drums penetrated the still, dark night. Cheers rose from the crowd as the rhythm intensified. Hot coals, evenly spread in a circle, had been burning for hours, and faces around the fire reflected its glow.

Dancers, women and men dressed in national folk garments, began to artfully enter the circle of fiery coals. Feet bare and eyes gazing upward, they carried icons of the Greek Orthodox Saints Constantine and Elena in their hands. This tradition, called *Anastenaria* (or *Nestinarstvo* in Bulgarian), commemorates a miraculous rescue that took place in the Middle Ages. The Church of Saint Constantine was on fire, and villagers braved the flames in order to save the lives of the saints trapped inside. All survived and the villagers emerged unscathed.[2]

---

[1] BrainyQuote.com.
[2] This particular dance should not be confused with people walking on fire for just a few seconds or similar rituals that may be practiced in other nations, as they are diverse in beliefs, origin, and purpose.

I was about ten years old when my parents and I attended the *Nestinarstvo* ritual at a coastal city near the Black Sea of Bulgaria. I was transfixed by the dancers. The musicians played three distinctive melodies with increasing cadence as the dance progressed. When dancers neared the outer area of the fire, the music slowed; as they entered the center, the beat quickened. When their feet touched the burning coals, the music hit its pinnacle. Only after the first dancer traversed the coals in the pattern of a cross did the rest of them enter the fiery circle. I marveled at their ability to maintain such intricate movements and poise for over an hour without burning their feet—or losing momentum and falling into the fire.[3]

THE FIRE REVEALS YOUR PURPOSE

When we begin to pursue our dreams and passions in connection to our calling, our lives are bound to go through times of fire. No matter how hard we try to ignore, reject, or escape these trials, they will not go away. We need to internally deal with the fire and address our unspoken fears. Then, at other times, externally deal with the impossibilities of our circumstances. Instead of sprinting to escape, we must learn how to move with the music—when to slow down, when to turn, and when to stop.

This is your fire walk, your dance on hot coals. And only you know the steps to your dance.

We can gather knowledge of the dance, but the drumbeat of life dictates its development. We learn the steps to our dance as we are forced to respond—whether in the stillness of a season or in the rapid rhythms of looming danger.
>   The way you respond
>   lets the fire reveal your purpose and
>   determines the direction and outcome of your future.

We will always have some form of an audience in life. People will most likely cheer us on according to our outward performance. But if we find our value and validation through people, we limit ourselves. We will only rise to the level of their perceptions. The same people who watched us dance will also watch us burn, if we lose our step and fall into the fiery coals.

In 60 AD, the Apostle Paul dealt with his own fire and audience when he was shipwrecked on the island of Malta while en route to Rome to face charges for preaching the Gospel.

---

[3] You may be surprised to know that science has an explanation for this seemingly impossible feat. Some argue it is mind over matter; others say it is the power of faith. Physics says it's all about heat capacity and thermal conductivity. For more information, see: "Lecture Demonstration Manual,"| UCLA Physics & Astronomy, http://www.physics.ucla.edu/demoweb/dod/firewalking.html.

But when Paul had gathered a bundle of sticks and laid them on the fire, a viper came out because of the heat, and fastened on his hand. So when the natives saw the creature hanging from his hand, they said to one another, "No doubt this man is a murderer, whom, though he has escaped the sea, yet justice does not allow to live." But he shook off the creature into the fire and suffered no harm. However, they were expecting that he would swell up or suddenly fall down dead. But after they had looked for a long time and saw no harm come to him, they changed their minds and said that he was a god (Acts 28:3–6).

In a matter of moments, Paul went from outlaw to idol in the eyes of his observers.

While we probably won't be judged to such extremes, at some point in life we will find ourselves on a journey we didn't want to take—whether falsely accused, struggling past a shipwreck in life, or pierced by the venom of another's jealousy, envy, or resentment. To be able to shake off something you cannot see in the natural will require you to find an answer to one important question: What is my "why"?

Philosopher Friedrich Nietzsche wrote, "He who has a why to live for can bear with almost any how."[4] Why did you step into your fiery coals and do what you are doing at the moment? If we can honestly answer why we do what we do (and even what we don't do), we can move forward with resilience and perseverance—even when the "how" seems far off, and even when no one is cheering us on.

Like the villagers who risked their lives to rescue the saints from the flaming church, when your why is greater than you, your life will have a greater meaning.

The why pushes you to action.

The why gives you confidence

to overcome your circumstances—

the fires you traverse: your invisible mentors.

THE FIRE REVEALS YOUR MOTIVES

Often after a speaking engagement, people come to my book table to share their comments about my message. Because I don't personally know most of my audiences, I don't usually consider the opinion of different individuals as truth that I should implement in my life. Every person will have an opinion, but not every person should be given permission to speak into our lives, especially if they don't know the core of who we are.

---

[4] Frankl, *Man's Search for Meaning*, 84.

Those product table encounters have strengthened the revelation of who I am and what I have gleaned from my invisible mentors after many years of dancing on hot coals. I have chosen to embrace the negative experiences and "impossibilities" as an opportunity to learn and grow, rather than allow them to destroy me. I have to know the motives of my heart and my work long before I step onto a stage to speak. I need to be grounded in that to appropriately receive with humility an accolade, a pat on the shoulder, a disapproving look, or a demeaning comment.

Humility is a crucial defense we must cultivate, for pride will take over by default. Pride begins in the heart and channels its way into our mind-set, altering our beliefs. It is selfishness rooted in an exaggerated opinion of ourselves, while treating others with inferiority.[5] Pride does not begin when we hear a compliment from someone; it begins with a choice about what we believe about ourselves, and it is often stimulated by the way we view our achievements. We process information by hearing, questioning, and then either dismissing it or adopting it as truth. When the formation of our "truth" is based solely on what others think of us, we will live anxious lives and our self-esteem will be dependent upon constantly pleasing people. This is *false humility* that breeds insecurity and creates low self-esteem. When we walk in true humility we are focused on others, teachable, and unafraid of what people think of us. We are great servants and self-sacrificing. We understand our value and purpose

without putting ourselves down,

without seeking external approval,

without living a life of pretense.

Moses was chosen by God to lead the children of Israel out of the bondage they experienced in Egypt and into their Promised Land of Canaan. On their journey, the character and beliefs of the Israelites were tested. Moses relied daily on God's guidance to direct His people on their journey, revealing the why and how of his authority. It was not so, however, for Korah, Dathan, Abiram and On, who came from the tribes of Levi and Reuben. They became self-appointed leaders with prideful spirits.

Presuming that they, too, could do the work of priest and leader, they came to Moses and Aaron to show their capabilities (Numbers 16:1–48). Korah and his 250 followers brought their own brass censers to the court of the Tabernacle. The censers in those days were used to carry burning incense before the Lord, which only a priest could do, according to God's instructions. While Moses allowed them to proceed with their actions, he warned them that disobeying God's command was a perilous experiment:

---

[5] For more about the differences between pride, true humility and false humility, visit "Living Bulwark," http://www.swordofthespirit.net/bulwark/truehumilitychart.htm.

"'Do this: Take censers, Korah and all your company; put fire in them and put incense in them before the Lord tomorrow, and it shall be that the man whom the Lord chooses is the holy one'" (v. 6–7). Because of their pride, selfishness, and rebellion, the fire of God's wrath fell on the altar and killed all 250 of them.

Upset with the consequences, the children of Israel complained against Moses and Aaron. Their actions brought on a plague that quickly spread among them. Moses interceded for the people by commanding Aaron to quickly grab a censer of burning incense and run among them, in effect offering a prayer of atonement for their prideful actions. Numbers 16:48 says that Aaron "stood between the dead and the living, and the plague stopped" (NLT). The rest of the story states that 14,700 of the Israelites died in just a few moments, in addition to those who died the day before (v. 49).

What would have happened if neither Moses nor Aaron had taken action? Could the plague have consumed the whole nation? Our world is in a similar state today, dying in the fire of its own pride and self-righteousness. We are directly influenced by the choices of others around us, resulting in a testing of our character, as the Israelites were tested in whom to follow. How will you respond? Will you choose to show compassion over taking offense, choose forgiveness over bitterness, love over hostility? Every situation will be different, but each difficult circumstance can be an invisible mentor that reveals your intentions and helps you find your purpose.

To identify our why—our motives—we can look to the ultimate example of the One "who knew no sin" yet was made to be sin for us, so "that we might become the righteousness of God in Him" (2 Cor. 5:21). That is Jesus! The purpose for which He came and lived on this earth—His why—was tested in the Garden the night before His crucifixion (Matt. 26:36–42).

Our why and our will to accept or reject it will be tested in the hours when no one is watching. When we may not have family or friends beside us who can understand. During the darkest moments when we either give in and give up, or press through and rise up.

Jesus chose to embrace death on the cross. "'O My Father, if it is possible, let this cup pass from Me; nevertheless, not as I will, but as You will'" (Matt. 26:39). The final reconciliation between God and humanity became fulfilled through Christ, so that our why in all that we do and all that we are

would be complete;

would be redeemed;

would be eternal.

Jesus' crucifixion, death, and resurrection was the ultimate dance over the hot coals of death and the flames of Hell. "Don't fear: I am First, I am Last, I'm Alive. I died, but I came to life, and my life is now forever. See these keys in my hand? They open and lock Death's doors, they open and lock Hell's gates" (Rev. 1:18, MSG). Where Jesus stands, death stops and life begins.

Like the Bulgarian dancers, if we, too, make our journey on this earth first through the cross, the flames and the hot coals will not burn us.

THE FIRE REVEALS YOUR WILLINGNESS

Little did I know that the experiences I had while living under the communist regime in Bulgaria would one day become my biggest invisible mentors. If I had not chosen to view them as such, I would never have learned how to dance over the coals of their brutality toward the human spirit.

From a biblical perspective, leadership appointed by God to govern, guide, and protect the people differs in its core purpose and style from leadership established by human governments. Oftentimes, these man-made positions dictate, suppress, and oppress human rights and freedoms.

When our spirit is broken and filled with shame, we are like sleepwalkers going through life.
We see without perceiving.
We hear without recognizing.
We walk without knowing where we are going.
We are detached from our emotions.
We have no expression of joy.

For the first sixteen years of my life, all I knew was conformity without the encouragement of individuality or personal development. The government mandated worship of the communist regime through organized and well-monitored marches, full control over a person's will, and brainwashing through fear and false information. Caught in the machine of communism, one would digress in darkness and soon believe it to be normal. To question or oppose the structure meant life in a concentration camp followed by death. Under communism, we were not allowed even to smile, especially in photos or at public events. Any emotion pertaining to joy and excitement was to be suppressed and replaced by sad and serious facial expressions. To believe in God was against the law; the Communist Party *was* god. It utterly destroyed anyone and anything that tried to steal its glory.

For forty-five years, until November 1989, my home country was under the dark veil of communism and influence of Russia. Allies of the former Soviet Union, we were the all-submissive sister, always ready to abide by every rule and adhere to every mandate.

Alive in our bodies,
dead in our souls,
we were marching to a dull, lifeless rhythm
without any purpose or choice.

Each day of high school I was required to arrive with shined shoes (no matter if it rained or snowed); show that my hands were clean and nails cut properly; have perfectly ironed clothes; and wear a special triangular red tie, knotted in a particular way under the crisp collar of my white shirt. The tie symbolized that we belonged to the Communist Party. Once I forgot to iron my tie before school. As a penalty, I was sent home and told to return with my parents, who were instructed to rebuke me and impress upon me the importance of presenting myself perfectly. This was not a boot camp to help improve self-discipline but a prison to eliminate individuality and identity by shaming any imperfection or weakness.

In spite of the photographer's insistence that we maintain a serious expression, it's hard to suppress the innate joy of a child's spirit. I'm on the far right, third row back.

I view these personal experiences under communism as inevitable trials, scorching me with their flames of imposed beliefs, circumstantial cruelties, and often daily difficulties. Strangely enough, the key to overcoming the negative impact of this oppression was my willingness to simply accept it and, later in life, to recognize it as an invisible mentor—a mentor that caused me to become resilient, extremely disciplined, and fearless.

When you choose to embrace even the hardships in your life, instead of detaching your emotions and attaching regrets, you are able to overcome them more quickly and utilize them in retrospect as positive character builders. Your strength will not be expressed in outward harshness but in inward substance, supported by the revelation of who Christ is in your life and of who you are in Him.

A significant story of a similar type of dictatorial leadership is found in the book of Daniel. Three Hebrew boys were captured by Babylonian invaders and brought to live under the rule of King Nebuchadnezzar. As part of breaking their will, their names were changed and they were required to accept the Babylonian culture and diet imposed upon them.

While their circumstances presented hardship, Shadrach, Meshach, and Abed-Nego chose to not lose hope or succumb to defeat. They did not surrender their will to those mandates but rather embraced the circumstances and consequences of their choices. Their faith in the true living God was tested to a new degree when they refused to bow to the favorite golden god of King Nebuchadnezzar. The penalty was death in the fiery furnace, which was made seven times hotter than usual for their punishment (Daniel 3:13–23).

They were willing to die for what they believed. That willingness came from understanding the why behind their purpose for living. Having a personal encounter with God and guarding the beliefs and traditions of their Hebrew culture silenced their fears and gave them courage. As they stood in the consuming fire of the furnace, Jesus was in the midst of them.

Even Nebuchadnezzar saw it—a fourth figure in the flames. He was astonished. Only three men had been thrown into the fire.

> *"Look!" [Nebuchadnezzar] answered, "I see four men loose, walking in the midst of the fire; and they are not hurt, and the form of the fourth is like the Son of God." Then Nebuchadnezzar went near the mouth of the burning fiery furnace and spoke, saying, "Shadrach, Meshach, and Abed-Nego, servants of the Most High God, come out, and come here" (Daniel 3:25–26).*

Jesus' presence neutralized the effect of the flames. Not only were the men untouched, but even their clothes had no smell of fire.

The king himself acknowledged the existence of God and promoted them to positions of prominence and authority in the province of Babylon:

> *Nebuchadnezzar spoke, saying, "Blessed be the God of Shadrach, Meshach, and Abed-Nego, who sent His Angel and delivered His servants who trusted in Him, and they have frustrated the king's word, and yielded their bodies, that they should not serve nor worship any god except their own God! Therefore I make a decree that any people, nation, or language which speaks anything amiss against*

the God of Shadrach, Meshach, and Abed-Nego shall be cut in pieces, and their houses shall be made an ash heap; because there is no other God who can deliver like this." Then the king promoted Shadrach, Meshach, and Abed-Nego in the province of Babylon" (Daniel 3:28–30).

Six principles of willingness, no matter the cost, are evident in the actions of these three brave Hebrew friends:

1. Willingness to *embrace* impossibilities
2. Willingness to *face* the fear
3. Willingness to *speak out* what they truly believed
4. Willingness to *testify* to the miracle
5. Willingness to *serve* in humility
6. Willingness to *live* in the present moment

The greatest miracles in your life are most likely to transpire while you are in the fire. The fire may try to bend your will, but it cannot break your spirit if you willingly embrace the trials, choosing to apply their lessons to your future decisions. Not allowing them to remain as simply external impossible situations.

THE FIRE REVEALS YOUR PRESENT MOMENT

Though our circumstances in life may not be as dramatic as what Shadrach, Meshach, and Abed-Nego faced, we will likely be confronted with the question of how willing we are to embrace impossibilities without denying the present moment of difficulty.

In Scripture, God always refers to Himself in first person, present tense: "I Am…"[6] Why? Because He is always in the present. Though we may fear our circumstances or current messes, they do not faze God. We may try to ignore them, forget them, or not deal with them, but we can be confident in God's ability to solve them. Therefore, He remains present with us in the midst of the trials, just as He was with Shadrach, Meshach, and Abed-Nego.

We have been created in the image of God, designed to experience life in present tense (Gen. 1:27; Eph. 4:24). When we deny our present experiences and live in past memories (good or bad) or idealistic ideas of what the future could look like, we keep ourselves from truly living as we were created to live. We go through the motions of

---

[6] Additional references about God as "I am" are found in the following Scriptures: Ex. 3:14; John 6:51; John 8:23, 58; John 8:12; John 10:9, 11; John 11:25; John 14:6; John 15:1; John 19:21; Acts 7:32, Acts 9:5; Rev. 1:8.

life, which after a while leave us numb and paralyzed, unable to perceive current situations accurately.

My dear friend and mentor Lou Tice gave me insight into experiencing true freedom by living in the "now moments." He said:

> *The present is all I ever have. There is never a time when my life is not "this moment." When I feel the uneasiness, anxiety, tension, stress, and worry—they are all forms of fear and are caused by too much future and not enough present. When I feel guilt, regret, resentment, sadness, bitterness, and all forms of non-forgiveness, they are caused by me focusing too much on the past and not enough on the present. The basic problem is the attachment of my mind to the past and the future and the denial of the now. My present is the key to my freedom. I do not let my mind create an obsession with the future as an escape from the present. My life is now!*

Take a moment to reread that statement. Adopt it into your life. Integrate it into your daily decisions. Today will never repeat itself; today is all you have.

Hear the drumroll of heaven beckoning you to take a step toward your new freedom of living in the now. Your life will become more authentic with each decision you make to live in the present. The fire will test your beliefs and expose your weaknesses, but it will solidify your character. When authenticity and character meet in the fire of your impossibilities, the façade of self-righteousness and self-indulgence will start to burn away. Each step through the fire becomes a part of your dance—filled with God's grace.

Your dance is different from mine. The cries of the people you hear and respond to are different from the ones I am called to rescue. But one thing we must share: proceeding forward with courage.

Courage to be present.

Courage to be ourselves.

Courage to risk for a higher cause.

Jesus is present in your now moments. You are not alone!

AN EXPERIENTIAL IMAGERY EXERCISE

You may color it and write a word inside of each hot coal that describes a current problem, fear, or unresolved experience—impossibility—that you would like to overcome and see as an invisible mentor. It is important to identify our fear of impossibilities in order to properly deal with them and overcome them.

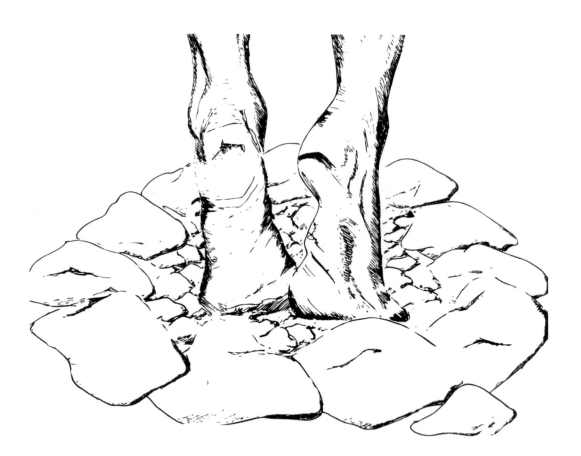

PRINCIPLE

Know the why behind what you do before you focus on the how. People will judge you according to the how, but confidence is built in the revelation of your why.

Take the time to define your WHY:

Why do you do what you do? What is your motivation?

Are the daily actions and beliefs you portray congruent with your inner thoughts and feelings?

If not, what are the hindrances to congruency in your life? List three practical steps to take toward overcoming them.

SURVIVING ON THE BUS RIDE OF LIFE

WITH YOUR BACKPACK LOCKED OUTSIDE THE DOORS

chapter

When we are no longer able to change a situation…
we are **challenged** to change ourselves."[1]

– VIKTOR FRANKL

OVERWHELMED,

DESPERATE,

DISTRAUGHT,

I dashed through the alley past the market and skidded around the icy street corner as I raced toward the bus station. Fear ran with me as my heart pounded hard against my chest. Fifteen minutes till the math test. *I can't be late! I have to make it!* I thought frantically. The first bus was full so I had to find a new route. The second bus arrived also full, but I had no choice—I leaped onto the bottom step just as the doors closed behind me. My backpack wasn't as fortunate. It was locked outside, pinning me in place against the door on the stairs.

[1] Frankl, *Man's Search for Meaning*, 117.

Public transportation in Bulgaria was always a challenge. Because I was shy and thin as a child, I was easily shoved around as people jockeyed for their own places on the bus. When the bus came to my stop, I would jump out as quickly as possible so I wouldn't fall out when the doors opened. Sometimes I succeeded; other times I would tumble out on my back from the push of the crowd. An occasional kind stranger might help me up.

I dreaded those bus rides, but they also took me to places I needed to be, wanted to be, and places I could not have otherwise gone. And, I imagined, to places I had not thought of yet.

Life happens like that.
Suddenly.
Surprisingly.

You finally make it. Even if it's just to the bottom step. Stuck on the destiny bus, ready to embark on your new adventure toward achieving your dreams. All your life you had waited for this moment to arrive. You pressed through! You paid the price! You outran the naysayers! In just a split second, your destination will open its doors to reveal your next season.

Ready for my first day of 1st grade with my new backpack and loving support of grandmother Mitka.

Just one problem...

The bus may be moving, and you may be on it, but everything you have relied upon, all you have proudly carried as life's value is in the backpack—
> your family,
> > your finances,
> > > your degrees,
> > > > your looks,
> > > > > your achievements,
> > > > > > your reputation
—trapped outside the doors of the bus ride of life. Out of reach.

Without access to our backpack of valuables, we feel weak, afraid, a sense of loss. All we've carried and achieved is still a part of us, but its tangible presence is gone. Our memories become our best friends because they comfort us. We try to hold on to them, unwilling to let them fade.

We all come to that place in life at some point.
>   Disarmed.
>   >   Frightened.
>   >   >   Exposed.

Relying upon external comfort for our happiness, we are forced to dig deep inside, to discover what we are really made of. To learn not only how to survive, but also how to jump out without falling flat on our backs once we arrive at our new destination.

The bus ride may not always be crowded. There will be pleasant moments when we feel relaxed and free to enjoy the liberty, space, conversations, and loving relationships of friends and family. Yet, in an instant, circumstances may change.
>   Hardship.
>   >   Death.
>   >   >   Loss.

Ironically, the difficult bus rides of life develop us the most and bring us to the place where new life and possibilities spring forth. They stretch us to deeper levels of self-awareness and responsibility and offer fresh perspective of our internal and external world. Unforeseen, unpredictable, and incredibly uncomfortable, this ride will either draw you to greater closeness and trust in God or trick you into the lie that He has abandoned you. The moments of self-doubt and fearful regret will stare you in the face, while you anxiously await a miracle escape.

The Bus Ride Through Unfairness and Darkness

The Old Testament story of Joseph has had a deep impact on my life and continues to inspire me. His journey, chronicled in Genesis 37–50, is significant in understanding the development of our own gifts, character, and perseverance, and how to handle success with humility and compassion.

The son of Jacob and Rachel, Joseph lived in the land of Canaan with his ten older half brothers, one younger brother, and at least one half sister. He was deeply loved and favored by his father, who gave him the coveted gift of a coat of many colors. Unfortunately, the jealousy of Joseph's brothers placed him on a "bus ride of life" for which he had no ticket and no time to prepare, to adjust his perceptions or hone his survival skills. He was seventeen when his brothers ripped his coat off his back, threw him into a pit, and sold him as a slave to passersby. His life went from a place of safety to a nightmare of slavery in moments.

For the next thirteen years, Joseph endured a degree of suffering that few of us have faced: betrayal, false accusations, forgotten promises, wrongful imprisonment. Joseph lived in a place of uncertainty and injustice. Like most of the narratives in Scripture, the actual emotions he experienced are not recorded. Reading between the lines, however, we quickly observe that with each trial he endured, his trust in the Lord was unwavering, and God's favor was always upon him.

His life turned completely around when at age thirty he interpreted a dream for Pharaoh and suggested a policy to prepare for the upcoming famine. Pharaoh and his servants came to believe that God spoke through Joseph. Just as suddenly as he had been thrown into the pit, his season of suffering ended—and he became second in command after Pharaoh! All the unfair circumstances had matured his character through discipline, self-control, faith, and patience. He came out of his prison experience able to reign as God's servant.

Perhaps you, too, can relate to what Joseph experienced during his darkest moments. When the bus ride of life propels us into the darkness and fear of the unknown, frantic questions crowd in. *Why is this happening to me? How long is this going to last? Why isn't God helping me? Does He even care?* We may question our ability to survive and even doubt our sanity.

We become overtaken by despair when our expectations for a better future die in our past disappointments. The feeling of unfairness can only be silenced with the voice of hope. When hope lives in the present, it carries a resurrection power that sustains our future.

Pay attention to the way you express your current experiences. Words of complaint, resentment, jealousy, and hatred toward God and others are evidence that you are believing the lie that you have been abandoned.

    Alone.

        Misunderstood.

            Forgotten.

Just like you and me, Joseph most likely had to remind himself of the truth that no matter how much had been stolen from him in the natural, "the LORD was with him; and whatever he did, the LORD made it prosper" (Genesis 39:23).

A modern-day example of a person who endured and overcame unfairness, darkness, and loss is Corrie ten Boom. Born on April 15, 1892, in Haarlem, Netherlands, near Amsterdam, she lived in the midst of World War II. Known as someone with a strong faith in Christ, she and her family helped many Jews escape the Holocaust by hiding them in a small room inside their home. Many years ago, I had the privilege of touring her house, now restored as a historical monument, and seeing firsthand the place where many lives were preserved because of the compassion and love of this godly woman and her family.

Together they endured the horrors of the Nazi concentration camp, yet their faith in God remained steadfast. In her book *The Hiding Place*, Corrie recalls a powerful statement made by her sister Betsie, who died in the camp: "'There is no pit so deep that [God's love] is not deeper still.'"[2] That is the truth and revelation that we must hold on to while going through a dark season.

Corrie lost her family, possessions, and her freedom. Yet the wisdom we obtain from her today came during her darkest times, when all she had was God and all she needed was Him. She often quoted Martin Luther, saying, "I have held many things in my hands, and I have lost them all; but whatever I have placed in God's hands, that I still possess."

Going through dark seasons will challenge your beliefs and your ability to be grateful when you feel cheated and falsely accused, having lost everything. You have the option to cling to your old comforts, accomplishments, and possessions, or, like Corrie ten Boom, let go of what is in your hands to hold only to the work God is doing in you. That means forgiving those who have wronged you, which unleashes love and hopeful optimism back into your heart.

THE BUS RIDE TO PATIENCE AND PERSEVERANCE

We don't have to pursue suffering; it has a way of finding us. There will be tears and moments when we want to quit. However, our current sufferings, no matter how big or small, expose our need for God. They can build confidence in us because He will meet us in the midst of our trials.

> Not only so, but we also glory in our sufferings, because we know that suffering produces perseverance; perseverance, character; and character, hope. And hope does not put us to shame, because God's love has been poured out into our hearts through the Holy Spirit, who has been given to us (Romans 5:3–5 NIV).

---

[2] Ten Boom, *The Hiding Place*, 150.

The word *perseverance* may not always be our favorite when it comes to enduring difficulties and opposition. *Steadfastness* is another word for standing strong under pressure. Both are connected to action on our part rather than idle waiting for a change to transpire.

When we find ourselves on the bus ride of perseverance, it is not by coincidence that we are there. We are given the opportunity to develop new survival skills. Each person responds differently to crisis and pressure. Some may be prone to become pushy, seek their own way, and be anxious, wanting all that God promised to come to pass miraculously after one prayer. Others may turn inward and become isolated and withdrawn, not wanting their weakness to be exposed. From a biblical perspective and from personal experience, nothing that produces lasting results comes to fruition in a blink of an eye. God may answer quickly on some occasions, but the difficult bus rides of life are challenges that mature and grow us the most.

In *Stand Against the Wind*, Erwin McManus writes, "When we hold out for the good, our perseverance is expressed as patience. When we hold on to the good, our perseverance is expressed as endurance…. Endurance holds on to the good. Perseverance finds the good in the worst of circumstances."[3]

Before Joseph was promoted to the position of what we would call today a prime minister, he had to grow in wisdom, character, and steadfastness of hope in God alone. While Joseph had many natural and spiritual gifts, without development of his character he could have easily abused the power given to him by exacting revenge against his family. When his brothers were finally faced with the truth, they were ashamed. Yet in his response to them, Joseph had no trace of bitterness or anger in his heart: "You intended to harm me, but God intended it for good to accomplish what is now being done, the saving of many lives" (Genesis 50:20 NIV).

Joseph's many years of suffering and loss produced patience and endurance—strength of character inside him.

Character to be able to handle the unjust circumstances.

Character to forgive when hatred would have been natural.

Character to embrace his gifts and hold on to his faith uncompromisingly.

Joseph was able to stand confidently before his brothers, filled with love, compassion, and forgiveness, because he knew God's promises for his life. He no longer had the

---

[3] McManus, *Stand Against the Wind*, 81–82.

need for an earthly coat of distinction. He had a revelation of who God was and His promises, and that was enough. He had embraced his heavenly coat of many colors.

We will know when this difficult season has accomplished its purpose in us when we can stand before our enemies—no matter who they are or what they have done to us— look them in the eye and instead of wanting revenge, thank them, bless them, accept them, and even love them.

Catching my own bus ride at age nineteen and arriving in the States alone was hard to fathom. My first stop took me to Tulsa, Oklahoma, where I was to begin my first year of Bible college at Victory Christian Center. My first three years were the most difficult. First, I had no family here, and, because I had only $100 of spending money, calls to my parents were once a month and only one minute long, just time enough to let them know I was alive. Second, I had to quickly learn the language so I could read my books and take the tests at school. And third, because I had no previous experience in adapting to a new culture, my mind was constantly filled with anxiety, creating a lot of stress in my body. Many nights, I would wake up wondering if I could make it on my own, completely disoriented about where I was.

Through my studies over the years and information I learned at The Pacific Institute in Seattle about how the mind functions, I am able to look back and understand what took place in my life at that time.[4] Our natural mind is designed to store all of our past experiences, good or bad, in the subconscious part of the brain. Each time we are faced with a decision, we pull from our past experiences, emotions, facts, and memories. We call these our "truths," based on the outcome of our previous experiences. If something similar from the past reminds us of the current situation in a positive way, we are inclined to move toward it and make a new decision based on a past experience. If, however, it has a negative connotation because of the outcome of that past situation, we will pull away from the new opportunity. Most of the time, we make decisions based on old experiences and habits we have stored in our subconscious, not based on the potential God has given us.

The creative subconscious part of our brain tries to adapt our current reality to our past perceptions and keep us sane by telling us that our "truth," good or bad, is who we are and that we must remain in that comfort zone for safety. The moment we step out of our comfort zone, we will naturally become forgetful and fearful. Our thoughts will quickly try to bring us back to a safety zone to restore a sense of peace. That is

---

[4] The following section contains information developed by The Pacific Institute in Seattle, Washington, and comprises a course called *Thought Patterns for High Performance 3.0*. The author of this book has been trained as a facilitator of the program. The information presented here has been paraphrased and modified by the author for the purpose of explaining the functionality and decision-making process of the human brain.

why most people will not step out and fully trust God or walk by faith. Our mind is constantly searching for factual data, while faith is "the substance of things hoped for, the evidence of things not seen" (Hebrews 11:1).

It's not that we don't have what it takes to make it but that we don't know how to draw on what has been entrusted to us. We are constantly trying to return to our comfort zone, even if it's not beneficial to us, because we do not believe we have the tools to survive the unknown experience. Fear has a stronger grip on us when we cannot identify it. But if the face of fear is known, and we can call it what it is, then our minds can override it. We safely recall similar past experiences, how we succeeded or failed, and what we learned. That helps us effectively overcome the current challenge.

Chapters 3 and 4 will discuss the renewing of our mind at length, but for now, remember that God has given you all you will ever need,[5] not in the backpack of external successes, but inside of you, woven into your nature. Your successes come as a byproduct of what is developed within you as a result of choosing courage over fear and patience over refusal to go through the challenges. Not only will we feel liberated when we learn how to lean on God, but we will have nothing to fear.

THE BUS RIDE ESTABLISHES GOD'S PROMISES FOR YOUR LIFE

Often during current impossibilities, you will not be able to make sense of all that is transpiring. That's okay. Take a deep breath! These pieces of the puzzle will connect more when you look back from the next destination in your life.

An important aspect of this stage is the adjustment of expectations. When we create a mental scenario of how we think God will act, we close off our senses, perception, and ability to recognize His presence and actual ways. Additionally, we allow discouragement to creep in when we do not see God at work according to our expectations.

People often view God as the problem if their circumstances don't turn around immediately. Right away we choose to place blame rather than take an opportunity to find an answer. Often we accuse God for what the enemy of our souls has done. John 10:10 describes Satan as a thief who comes to steal, kill, and destroy. If our lives look like a field of destruction, let's accurately determine who is at work in that situation. If we blame God for something that is either our responsibility or was caused by the enemy, we will not apply the right solution to resolve the situation. We will open the doors to deceit, blindness, and more fear in our lives.

---

[5] 2 Peter 1:3.

In addition, when we blame external circumstances, not only do we lose control over the situation, but we also reinforce a wrong belief that the outside world has more control over our inside reality than it really does. It's like being stuck inside a house with a doorknob only on the outside of the door. The outside reality has greater implications and control over you than the inside reality.

The opposite is true. When our inside world—what's in our minds, such as beliefs, core values, and truths—is in control of our decisions, it will cause the external reality to surrender to our internal reality. It is very important to choose what we believe and what we put in our minds. Here is the reason: when the internal doesn't match the external, a war happens in our emotions and thoughts. As a result, our bodies experience greater levels of anxiety and stress.

Personally, I have chosen to *never* look at God as my problem. Rather, He is *always* my answer and solution to every impossibility. He is my only absolute in life. If the Word of God states that He is for us and not against us; if He is our Redeemer; if He has loved us with an everlasting love[6], then our truth about Him must be based not on temporary experiences but on the solidity of His character throughout the Old and New Testament.

The moment that truth becomes an absolute fact in your mind and you believe it, you will always run to Him for comfort, answers, and strength. If you remain shaky and uncertain in your beliefs about God's character and who He is, then you will approach every circumstance wondering, *Where is God in this?* rather than in the security of knowing, *Because God is with me and for me, I trust Him to find the answers to these problems. I am confident in His ability to resolve the impossible!*

Having to survive on my own and living in poverty, especially during my first few years in the U.S., was either going to be an invisible mentor in my understanding of God's faithfulness and promises or cause me to doubt His voice.

I distinctly remember one hot, muggy afternoon in Oklahoma when the bus that provided food for the needy came to the apartment complex where most of the students were housed. Waiting in line to receive free groceries, I struggled to hold back my tears. A sense of humiliation overwhelmed me and I felt the spirit of degradation clothing me in its robe of shame. The impact of all my years under the yoke of communist oppression, now combined with the experience of exposed poverty, were choking me. As I approached the bus, I tried to compose myself, hoping no one could see inside to my screaming, fearful thoughts.

---

[6] Romans 8:31; Isaiah 44:24; Jeremiah 31:3.

Clutching my two bags of groceries, I stood on the street corner until the bus was out of sight. In spite of my fear, I wanted to stay in this moment, to not quickly dismiss the avalanche of uncontrolled emotions. They were there for a reason. Perhaps because I felt forgotten, perhaps because I felt alone. Even so, I had a fierce determination to survive the internal and external challenge this impossibility presented.

On that day, July 28, 1995, I made up my mind that not only was I going to remain on that bus ride of life, but I was also going to develop the resilience to jump off quickly when the doors opened so that I would not be crushed under the doubting voices that questioned my vision and destination.

That was my moment in establishing what I was going to believe about God and His promises in my life. I realized afresh that all I had was Him, and all I needed to learn was how to allow Him to save me.

> To save me from my fears of the unknown.
> To save me from the false belief that I was not enough.
> To save me from my perfectionism.
> To save me from myself.

That day was my first step on the journey to true freedom. My shame lifted because I chose to release my own inability to Him, the One who was to clothe and feed me. Deep peace enveloped me that night and I knew I was going to make it—that Jesus knew every single step on the way, and He was not going to let me down.

God's promises are established in our lives through a revelation found only when we come to the end of ourselves and detach from the earthly approval of people or ownership of positions and possessions. A time will come when what you have in your backpack no longer owns you but you own it, if you hold out long enough to get through the next stop on our bus ride.

THE BUS RIDE THROUGH SHAME TO AUTHENTICITY

Often we are more prone to give help than to receive it. We have difficulty asking for help, especially when we have nothing to give in return. Those are the times we feel most vulnerable. This perhaps is the most pivotal lesson of the bus ride to learn and adopt in order to walk in complete freedom. In her book *Daring Greatly*, Brené Brown defines vulnerability as "uncertainty, risk and emotional exposure."[7]

Vulnerability isn't good or bad: It's not what we call a dark emotion, nor is it

---

[7] Brown, *Daring Greatly*, 33.

always a light, positive experience. Vulnerability is the core of all emotions and feelings. To feel is to be vulnerable. To believe vulnerability is weakness is to believe that feeling is weakness.... Vulnerability is the birthplace of love, belonging, joy, courage, empathy, and creativity. It is the source of hope, accountability, and authenticity. If we want greater clarity in our purpose or deeper and more meaningful spiritual lives, vulnerability is the path.[8]

The most beautiful relationship we can have with our Creator is to stand vulnerable before Him—confident, free from all shame. Shame thrives on believing the lie that we are alone. That is what happened to Adam and Eve when they first disobeyed God.

Genesis 3:7–11 tells us that Adam and Eve sinned and then realized they were naked.
    Therefore, they hid.
        They covered themselves among the trees of the Garden.
            They were ashamed.

Their disobedience opened the door for shame to enter humanity. The shame that covered Adam and Eve is the same that covers us today—the sense of feeling unloved and unworthy, never being good enough. When we act out a belief of "not good enough," we hide behind outward perfectionism. That is what our backpack—all we have and possess and our identity in life—has given us for many years: a false sense of comfort through external appearance, accomplishments, money, connections. We find ourselves
    hiding,
        cowering,
            afraid.

The good news is that shame cannot survive in the light; it only thrives in darkness. Fear brings darkness and feeds the lie that because we need help, somehow we are weak. This lie will keep us living behind a mask of pretentiousness, which also leads to arrogance and a tendency to belittle others who are in need of help.

If we believe that asking for help is weakness, then feelings of shame and inadequacy will cause us to create an emotional barrier. We will either detach our emotions to minimize the pain or we will attach false beliefs about ourselves or God.

The key is to realize that with God you are enough! You must choose to believe that you are enough to be loved and to love without the external achievements. Just for who you are. You are enough as a person created in God's image, who carries His value

---

[8] Ibid., 34.

and dignity. God looked for Adam and Eve the moment they disobeyed.[9] He was not ashamed of them. And to this day, He is looking for us, to deliver us from our own fears and the lies that would try to steal our relationship with Him.

This is your moment to stop and embrace this truth! This is a part of your new journey. Sometimes you will need to pause and remind yourself of it, even daily, or moment by moment.

The second way to make truth become part of you is by journaling it and sharing your experience of overcoming with others. Most people don't take the time to process their thoughts or feelings. If you are afraid of your own thoughts, you will be imprisoned by the unresolved past and crippled by the unknown future. If you are afraid of your emotions, which travel much faster than your thoughts,[10] you will find yourself ruled by them, rather than using them as a source of strength and comfort. When we ignore what we fear, it does not go away. We empower it to enslave us.

During my student days in Tulsa, I often walked to Walmart to escape for a few hours and dream of items I could one day purchase. I would walk up and down the aisles, envisioning the day when I would be able to help adults and children who didn't have anything. I always carried a pen and paper with me in case I met someone at the store who would want to be my friend. And I did! I developed a mailing list comprised of fifty strangers I met at stores and gas stations. I would approach people and ask if they wanted to be my friends and if I could have their mailing addresses and phone numbers because I was starting an international nonprofit organization and needed people to receive my newsletter.

What might have scared me or caused me to think of failing actually fueled greater confidence and liberation from the shame of "not good enough." I learned to ask for help without the feeling of degradation because I was becoming more secure in the revelation of who I was, and God's freedom in my life was becoming more prevalent. After all, everything in my personal backpack at that time was safely locked out, not just a street or a state away but on another whole continent. Yet the greatest strengths in my life were formed inside of me during that season.

When we learn how to freely receive help without shame, we are better able to offer help too, without using it to feel better about ourselves. Brené Brown described it eloquently during an interview with Oprah:

---

[9] Gen. 3:8–9.

[10] "There is evidence that the limbic system functions 80,000 times faster than the thinking brain's cerebral cortex." Cooper, *The Other 90%*, 21–22.

When you cannot accept and ask for help without self-judgment, then when you offer other people help, you are always doing so with judgment. Because you have attached judgment to asking for help. When you extract worthiness for helping people, that's judgment.... When you don't extract worthiness and you think, "I'm just helping you because one day I'm going to need help," that's connection. That's vulnerability.[11]

The bottom line is that we need one another and most importantly we need God. When we allow Him to meet the needs in every area of our lives, we create a healthy dependence on Him and He heals us internally. When He is replaced with anyone else—a person, a possession, a situation—that unhealthy dependence won't meet our needs in a lasting way. The external treasures we carry in our backpack are short-lived. Only what's being developed inside of us can be carried into eternity.

THE BUS RIDE INTO COMPASSION

A few years passed and I was now on a new bus ride.

    This time I was not in Bulgaria.

        I was not in Tulsa,

           I was in Brooklyn.

I was visiting Metro World Child, the largest Sidewalk Sunday School in the world. Their inner-city outreaches throughout the Bronx, Brooklyn, and greater New York City introduce children and teens to the Gospel through interactive Bible teachings, activities, and games. Being picked up by Metro's buses and going to a safe environment is a definite highlight of the week for the kids.

On that particular morning, a chubby little boy with dirty clothes and messy hair hopped on the bus. As soon as he saw me, he asked to sit next to me. Once he held my hand, he didn't want to let it go. After the activities were over and we were back on the bus, his little eyes filled with tears.

"What's wrong? Did you lose your prize?" I asked.

"No," he said, "I just don't want to go back home. I wish you were my mommy. Mine doesn't love me. She beats me, and I am so alone."

My heart broke as I felt his pain. All of a sudden the separated dots in my life began

---

[11] Brown, "Are You Judging Those Who Ask for Help?" YouTube Video, Oprah's Life Class.

to connect. I remember it vividly to this day. As I leaned over and held him close, the Lord whispered into my heart.

> *If you had never gone through the season of being on the bus that fed the poor people when you lived in Tulsa…if you had never been the one who fell on the street and had people trample you in Bulgaria…if you had never gone through those times when you had nothing and no one to encourage you but Me, then right now, at this very moment, you would not have compassion and empathy for this child.*

> *All those moments when nothing made sense, I was still there providing for you; I was with you at all times. Yet, those times I didn't deliver you suddenly but let you experience the journey created the character, the resilience, and the inner strength to know that you are enough to be loved and enough to love the unlovable.*

That was one of my big defining moments. From that day on, I did not look at my challenges the same way. They were no longer problems. They were now my invisible mentors. Through them I learned the freedom to ask for help, to give help, and to willingly receive.

I was no longer stuck on the bus with my backpack locked out of reach. Now my external and internal experiences were integrated, and my new backpack was filled with joy, tears, prayers, abundant life, and freedom. I was finally prepared to feed the people God would bring into my life because I had chosen to stay on the bus ride that taught me how best to know the heart of God and the heart He had placed in me.

The bus ride of life will take you many places. Numerous stops along the way will let some people step out of your life and allow others to enter. At times, new vistas will enchant you with their beauty and possibilities; other times, the landscape may seem perilous and frightening. If you learn to live in complete dependence on God, you will find freedom and joy in the journey. Freedom to sustain any type of loss, freedom to give with sincerity, and the contentment of knowing that all you need you already have. No one can take it away. It is now locked inside of you!

AN EXPERIENTIAL IMAGERY EXERCISE

You may color it and write one word inside each compartment of the backpack that describes what you have relied on in life for significance and success. Identify those things that are no longer accessible to you (a person, situation, possessions, etc.) and write them on the page next to the bus.

PRINCIPLE

The bus ride of difficult circumstances either defines you or you define it. People may label you according to the backpack of your achievements, but only what is developed inside of you on this bus ride will have eternal implications in loving others and fulfilling God's purposes for your life.

Take the time to think and journal about the current journey of your life:
What is being built inside of you on this new bus ride?

Describe yourself without your external achievements:
Who are you on the inside? What makes up your core?

In what areas of your life are you still struggling with shame?

Are you comfortable asking for help? If not, what practical steps do you need to take in order to let go of the need to be in control and be able to graciously receive?

152 STAIRS TOWARD CONTENTMENT

AND AN ELEVATOR IS NOT AN OPTION

chapter

> The **heights** by great men reached and kept
> Were not attained by sudden flight,
> But they, while their companions slept,
> Were toiling upward in the night."[1]
> – HENRY WADSWORTH LONGFELLOW

"READY. SET. GO-O-O!" my girlfriend shrieked, waving her arms as fast as she could, piercing my ears. It seemed as if the whole city became still, breathlessly awaiting the winner of the 152-stair race. That's right! I was competing against the neighbor boy in the fastest sprint race imaginable! Leaping from the top stair at the entrance of my front door, I bounded over four or five stairs at a time, focused and determined. The rest of the neighborhood kids followed us with loud cheers. I felt on fire. Barely able to catch my breath, I gave one last push...and the finale! Cheers filled the air even louder than before.

---

[1] Longfellow, "The Ladder of St. Augustine," HWLongfellow.org.

"I did it! I WON the race!" In less than two minutes, I had run the course: the first set of 34 cement stairs that divided my house and the first main street; then the second set of 82 stone stairs; and across the second street, a granite stairway of 36 stairs that led to the city center.

I was seven years old.

Happy.

Free.

Nothing could hold me back.

Running up and down these stairways was like taking a deep breath and exhaling only when my foot hit the last stair. My favorite exercise! Sometimes, during snowstorms when no one was out to shovel, the stairs became a hillside. I would sit on a plastic bag and fearlessly slide down the slopes to the city center.

In all of my stairway adventures—even climbing back from the city center, 152 stairs home—never for one moment did I think I needed an escalator or elevator for what my body was conditioned to do. I never viewed the stairs as obstacles. They were, instead, a vehicle that connected me to my future destination and brought me safely home to my family, my belongings, and Grandma's delicious cooking.

The runs strengthened my muscles, created a healthy heart rate, and stirred hunger in me, especially after a long day.

They developed my sense of curiosity.

Challenged my thinking.

Created awareness for danger.

Slowed me down when I was climbing up, and

sped me up when sliding down the snowy slopes.

But the stairs were not a place to stay. To live there would be foolishness—no one would, unless they were homeless and it was their only option for survival.

MEMORIES CONNECT OUR PAST AND FUTURE

The stairways of my childhood story can represent different seasons in life—seasons filled with bad and good; sad and happy; problems and solutions; absence and presence; rejection and acceptance; death and resurrection.

Each challenge and each victory is like a stair.

Each stair becomes a memory.

And each memory connects to our past

and draws out strength for our future.

Memories, like stairs, cannot provide permanent shelter for our souls. In fact, they have the potential to mislead us, because they are based upon our personal observation. Yet they define who we will become. If we fear our memories, they will not be useful stairs that help us move from place to place but will stall us on one step like homeless beggars. If fear is our interpreter, we will have misconceptions of the past.

We can't escape a dreadful memory by simply focusing on the future, for it will follow us like a shadow, pointing out our imperfections to trap us in our past reality. Once experiences occur, we can't just forget them. Someone or something will awaken them at different times throughout our lives. Perhaps through the scream of a heartache, or through joyful laughter that takes us back to moments when we were carefree and unashamed.

In the field of psychology, *memory* is described as the process of maintaining information our brain allows to enter our mind. It registers information by first receiving it, then storing it in a long-term or short-term compartment, depending on the value we place upon it. Then it recalls that information—our memories—in response to activity or circumstances.[2]

Think of this process of storing and retrieving memories like the stairways I described running as a child.

Most of the city was built on a mountain, and my house was built on a rock. So, stairs leading to the houses were generally created out of the mountain stone. They were uneven. Some were higher, others shorter; some were slanted, some were chipped. But my friends and I were comfortable playing on those stairs. If we needed something, we quickly ran back to the house. The same is true with our memories. When we first begin to build them, they look like the stony stairs— imperfect, uneven, yet somewhat safe because they are familiar.

The second set of stairs had concrete poured over the rock. They looked nicer

My home in Bulgaria, starting point for childhood adventures.

---

[2] Heberle, "Three Stages Of Memory," Study.com.

and it was easier to walk up and down, even during winter storms. That stairway is like the memories we try to cover up—we sugarcoat them so we can better tolerate them.

The last set of stairs that led to the city center was built to give the illusion of grandeur, suggesting that the rest of the road leading up the hill would be as polished and smooth. But only the first few stairs were shiny marble. As soon as you crossed the street, the second stairway—concrete and uneven—became visible.

Often in our daily lives, we wear and share our best memories very freely. Shallow conversations that carry a certain spark, with enough "polished marble" to cause people to admire our lives. Yet the closer we connect to someone, the more they see our second set of stairs: the challenging, hurtful times from our past that we have hidden beneath a veneer of cement.

And let's not even mention how protective we are of the uneven stairs in our lives— the cruel moments that deeply wound us. The imperfections of these stairs expose us. Often, they are much too difficult to climb, other times, too challenging to descend without holding the railing. Yet they connect our past to our future. Diverting attention from them will not remove their reality from our subconscious mind.

When a memory from the past has not been properly integrated into our present, it cripples our emotional development instead of giving strength to our future. To live life ashamed of the past—because of what we have done or what others may have done to us—is like living life stuck on the stairs. Haunted with memories of regret, bitterness, unforgiveness, and resentment, eventually our soul will wither.

In order for the pain from our past to heal properly, it must be given future purpose. Otherwise, the memory will remain as unresolved pain and keep us detached from a healthy emotional future. With unresolved pain, we easily form a misleading picture about the outside world and ourselves and then live in the grip of its bondage.

Memories Create a Stairway to Safety

George Bonanno, a clinical psychologist at Columbia University's Teachers College, has spent nearly twenty-five years studying the differentiating factors in the mind of a person when trauma occurs. Why are some people better in dealing with adversity than others? Bonanno's research reveals that the answer lies in the person's perception of the event rather than in the circumstance itself. An article in *The New Yorker* describes his theory:

> *"Events are not traumatic until we experience them as traumatic," Bonanno [says]. "To call something a 'traumatic event' belies that fact." He has coined a different term: PTE, or potentially traumatic event, which he argues is more accurate. The theory is straightforward. Every frightening event, no matter how negative it might seem from the sidelines, has the potential to be traumatic or not to the person experiencing it.[3]*

The word *perception* has a fundamental meaning in this particular research. Perception has the magnetic power to simultaneously create two opposite views in our minds. Depending on how we choose to respond in a situation, our perception will either hold the pain within the memory, or it will release resilience through actively focusing our attention on an answer to overcome trauma—thus creating a positive stored memory.

Incredibly insightful for our study on memory is the story of Naomi and her daughter-in-law, Ruth, from the Book of Ruth. It reveals God's redemptive plan at work, for us as individuals as well as all of humanity, despite our bad choices and mistakes. During a time when the Israelites were experiencing extreme famine in the land, Elimelech chose to take his wife Naomi and their two sons to the neighboring country of Moab. Natives of Judah dwelling in the town of Bethlehem, they left God's Promised Land and settled into a nation with a pagan culture. However, Elimelech broke the covenant established between him and the Lord by seeking outside provision. He did it out of fear and lack of trust in God. His decision is often compared to the life of a carnal believer who may intellectually know God but has not encountered His presence and power in order to have a heart transformation and revelation.

Naomi followed the lead of her husband and suffered the consequences of their disobedience. Her husband died in Moab, then ten years later, her two sons passed away. Left as a widow, her "present" was swallowed by her anger and bitterness. Every day, when looking at the faces of her two Moabite daughters-in-law, Naomi found herself living in a land of

     regret,

          resentment, and

               unresolved internal conflict.

The memories of the land of Judah were still very much a part of her. A sense of hope was triggered in her spirit when she heard how the Lord had blessed her people. And she chose to remember the good.

     She remembered who she used to be.

          She remembered God's covenant promises.

---

[3] Konnikova, "How People Learn to Become Resilient," NewYorker.com.

> And she made a decision to return to her past
> in order to restore hope for her future.

Sometimes we need to step backward in order to move forward. This was the case with Naomi. Forgiveness was not *an* option; it was the *only* option to stay alive. It is not easy to forgive, especially if the harmful consequences in our lives are a result of someone else's choices. In this case, Naomi had to forgive her husband first and then forgive herself for all the "I should have done… I could have done… so I would be…" These three sister words, "I should, I could, I would," are a sure sign of a regretful mind without intention to change. That is the land of Moab. Outside of where God dwells, a land where our own mind-set and self-righteousness become a god to us through unrealistic wishful thinking.

What Naomi heard in her spirit unlocked the remembrance of who she truly was. At times we can get so lost, so far removed from the original plan we felt God had for our life, that it takes someone else to remind us of who we are, where we came from, and where we are going. And as we truly begin to listen, the sound of hope will rise again in our spirit.

> No decision is permanent.
> No destination is final.
> No past mistake can be greater than
> God's redemption plan for our lives.

When I read the Book of Ruth, I see a woman whose memories of her land triggered gratitude impregnated with hope through a revelation. Gratitude is like opening the windows of our soul for fresh air to come in. It is the air of forgiveness, which we must inhale and exhale in order for oxygen to flow back into the cells of our memories. Bitterness, on the other hand, holds us captive, causing us to become hopeless and live in despair. It robs the joy from our present and gives our memories falsified information about our external world. Our memories will lie to us when infected by the virus of unforgiveness.

If Naomi had stayed in that mind-set, she would have suffocated and died. We don't know if she realized all she would face in the desert and upon return to her homeland or whether she leapt without thinking, but she and her two daughters-in-law, Orpah and Ruth, took the road to Judah.

MEMORIES HEAL THROUGH EMPOWERING EMOTIONS

Emotional healing and behavioral change don't happen overnight. While it all begins with a decision, there will be a process. The route that corrects history and allows our future to flourish is through the desert. We must travel on the same road that led us to our mistakes in order to heal our memories. But wrong beliefs, bad habits, unrealistic expectations, and negative attitudes do not change through a copy and paste of the same old patterns into our memories. Healing transpires when a brand-new belief replaces an old one. In psychology it's called creating a replacement picture; biblically it relates to the renewing of our mind.[4]

In my early childhood years, all my classmates were involved in practicing a certain form of witchcraft. Looking to experience the supernatural in a culture of suppression, we had many formulas with memorized words. No emotions attached—all we had to do was repeat our formulas and the "spirit realm" would open up before us. We thought we were calling the spirit of a dead person to write and speak through us, but we were actually opening the doors wide for demonic powers to work through our lives. As a result, I lived in mental bondage and was tormented by constant fear, though I did not realize the correlation at the time.

When I came to know Christ, the biggest difference I encountered was that transformation took place in my life without a formula. I only needed faith to believe. "But to all who believed Him and accepted Him, He gave the right to become children of God" (John 1:12 TLB). In witchcraft, I experienced external control, as if someone was taking over my internal being. It was not so with Jesus. When I heard the Gospel for the first time at sixteen, shortly after the fall of communism, I asked Jesus to show me if He was more powerful than what I had already seen. I knew that the supernatural existed, but one thing I couldn't do through witchcraft was to heal myself. I had suffered pain in my stomach for many years, and if Jesus was real I needed Him to heal me first before I could fully trust Him.

Not only did the pain leave instantly, but so did the fear and voices that haunted my dreams at night. I felt complete peace for the first time. God works in a unique way with each individual, but this was my experience. The presence of God did not overpower me from the outside; He empowered me from the inside by giving me the freedom to believe in Him. There was no idle repetition; the feeling of joy, of security, of acceptance automatically created a new experience in me. The emotion of love entered the core of my mind and instantly changed it. Therefore, I believed.

Transformation also happens in our belief through the power of emotion. As I mentioned in Chapter 2, our emotions travel exponentially faster than our thoughts.

---

[4] "Don't copy the behavior and customs of this world, but let God transform you into a new person by changing the way you think. Then you will learn to know God's will for you, which is good and pleasing and perfect" (Romans 12:2 NLT).

They are the fertilizer to our memories. Emotions either deeper root our thoughts or uproot them. Something we read that does not produce an emotional response within us will be quickly forgotten and not change the neurons of our mind, so it will not change our behavior. James 1:22–24 in *The Message* Bible puts it this way:

> *Don't fool yourself into thinking that you are a listener when you are anything but, letting the Word go in one ear and out the other. Act on what you hear! Those who hear and don't act are like those who glance in the mirror, walk away, and two minutes later have no idea who they are, what they look like.*

As you read the Word of God, take time to meditate on it. If you choose to adopt it as truth in your life, it will lead to action that generates hopeful and empowering emotions. Then you can go through the desert of life with clarity of purpose and without looking back in regret.

For Ruth and Naomi, the desert was not just a flight over. Though Ruth 1:19 gives us only a one-sentence explanation of that journey, most likely it took nearly four months, traveling by foot through treacherous circumstances.

> History always records the end and the beginning.
> Yet it's in the journey that we count our losses
> and feel the empowerment of the victory.

We must have the determination to heal the past by facing the reality of both our present and our future. Naturally, some of us will begin the process but stop halfway through if our purpose behind the journey is not properly defined. Though Orpah and Ruth both joined Naomi, shortly thereafter, Orpah returned to Moab, while Ruth clung to her mother-in-law:

> *"Don't ask me to leave you and turn back. Wherever you go, I will go; wherever you live, I will live. Your people will be my people, and your God will be my God. Wherever you die, I will die, and there I will be buried. May the Lord punish me severely if I allow anything but death to separate us!" When Naomi saw that Ruth was determined to go with her, she said nothing more (Ruth 1:16–18 NLT).*

The story reveals a beautiful covenant as we read how Ruth left her past, all that she knew and had, in order to embrace her future. Naomi was very much a part of that past. As they traveled together, Naomi's experiences gave Ruth the confidence and determination to press through, to change and to overcome not only while going through the desert, but also as she adopted the new culture of the Israelites. She drew upon lessons from the past for the strength needed in her future. This brought forth healing from the loss and the pain. Historically she became a part of the lineage through which Christ came to this earth.

At the same time, Naomi left her present filled with mistakes, bitterness, and resentment to travel back into her past, empowered through the hope of her future. This was her second journey through the desert. The first time was marked with Elimelech's disobedience to God. This time, she traveled back with her redemptive future (Ruth), against the cultural beliefs at the time that deemed widows weak and incapable of making it on their own.

So often we look for the easy route, the detour that takes us around the desert. But this path bypasses the process of character development. Only the difficult journey through the past yields victory for our future. Unless, like Naomi, we have felt, smelled, heard, and seen the desert, we have no authority over it.

God's promises are tested in your desert walks. They sustain you and support you under pressure and enable you to rise to the next challenge. Once a new positive memory is developed, it sends a signal to your mind that you have overcome the impossibility. In this way, you have been transformed from a victim to a victor.

> What you tell yourself while in the desert
> will manifest in your behavior when
> you reach your promised land.

ACCURATE MEMORIES PAINT A BRIGHT FUTURE

Our lives are a painting comprised of the colors of beliefs about ourselves and our external world. Different seasons, victories, accomplishments, or challenges mixed with disappointments create a variety of pictures—memories—displayed with our life's painting. When the pigments of past and present blend, they become beautiful, expressive, and powerful—unstoppable. They create new hues for the canvas of our future. Our memories and the way we perceive and use them in our daily lives give us the paint for our canvas. If we don't like the current picture, we must change the colors. We need to be aware, however, of its intricate process and the part we play during the change.

Just as we hear God's promises, we can also hear lies from the enemy—often in the words of others. By the time Naomi and Ruth reached Bethlehem, rumors had already spread of their return. Sometimes your past will reach your future prematurely and try to discount you before you even reestablish yourself. All of a sudden, the courage

Naomi exercised in the desert was being undermined by the chattering voices of the women in town. Her mind-set relapsed and her spirit became poisoned and sick to the point that she changed her name from Naomi, "pleasant one," to Mara, which means bitter (Ruth 1:20).

What was happening to Naomi? As she began to change, the negative voices of her past were awakened. We are adept at recalling our bad behavior and thoughts and often meditate on what we have done wrong, rather than on our victories. Properly directed, memories can enhance the beauty of our journey, but memories inaccurately perceived can hide that beauty. We don't realize that

> what we fear, we become.
> > What we reject, we recreate.
> > > What we embrace, we overcome.
> > > > What we see, we learn from.
> > > > > What we learn creates new pictures.

Here is the critical key to help us overcome the voices from the past: we must clearly see the image of who we are becoming and consistently reinforce it in our mind-set in order for it to become the predominant picture. By intentionally embracing the truth of who we are, our mind will begin to replace the old images of defeat and adopt the new.

That is why it's important that we do not underestimate the power of the spoken word. Just as God spoke and the universe came into existence (Genesis 1:7), He has given us the ability to create a new reality, a new future through our words. What we tell ourselves through our daily self-talk creates change inside of us only if we believe it. Through consciously recalling and focusing on the memories of victory or achievements along with the feelings encompassing them, we embed a new internal image into our creative subconscious and enhance the beauty of our life's painting.

> Victories create joy.
> > They create confidence.
> > > They pull back the dark curtains of life
> > > > so we can once again see with
> > > > > clarity and accuracy.

The longer we continue to paint with colors dipped in our victories, the more our internal view of ourselves begins to change and become our new normal.

Albert Bandura, the originator of social learning theory, discovered in his research,

"Most people pass through their accomplishments too quickly and too lightly to have them make any change in their image of reality."[5]

Lou Tice, who worked with Bandura in developing curriculum around this theory, states the following:

> When you do something successful, have you ever said, "Oh, it was nothing. I had nothing to do with it? It was an accident." You must elevate your image.... When you are doing something successful, you must reiterate it. You want to remember it. You want to reflect on it. You need to assimilate it. You need to let yourself feel it. That's what high-performance people do. They let themselves feel their success.[6]

Three words of importance from that research help us properly paint our future with our past victories:

reflection,

assimilation, and

reiteration.

The Apostle Paul explains it this way: "By no means do I count myself an expert in all of this, but I've got my eye on the goal, where God is beckoning us onward—to Jesus. I'm off and running, and I'm not turning back" (Phil. 3:14 MSG). This doesn't mean rejecting, blocking out, or suppressing the past. The way to move forward into God's promises for your future is to give the past a purpose to live in the future. Then you shift your focus from looking back and trying to escape it to reflecting and assimilating the new beginnings and past successes. At that time, the canvas of your life's painting becomes filled with the new colors of future victories.

THE REDEMPTION PROCESS OF OUR MEMORIES

In my childhood home, we had many people come to stay and dine with us. The doors were always open to everyone.

Neighbors.

Friends.

Relatives.

Everyone was welcome.

In addition, my mom was a clothing designer, and her students would come to visit and learn how to make beautiful clothes. Of course, I loved all the activities and food

---

[5] The Pacific Institute, *Thought Patterns for High Performance 3.0*, 86.
[6] Ibid.

we made for our guests. Despite the darkness surrounding us, our house was a refuge for us and our visitors.

But one day something happened. During a challenging pregnancy with my sister, my mom went into premature labor in her last trimester. In the middle of the night, my dad took her to the hospital, where my mom gave birth. My sister lived only two days. I was eight years old at the time. To this day, I clearly remember the feeling of loss as my mom and dad returned from the hospital. No matter how much they tried to hide it, the sadness and grief were evident on their faces. The same house that had been filled with life was now quiet. Death had taken over our thoughts.

I went to bed and cowered under the blankets. The window above me was open and I could see the stars shining brightly. I kept looking out, thinking, *I know there is someone out there, beyond this dark sky, who knows me, who knows my pain, who loves me.*

God tenderly reached through the darkness into the pain of my present and spoke hope into my future that night. Though I was unaware of who He was at the time, I knew deep in my heart that there must be more to life than what the Communist Party had made us believe. That same night, with tears streaming down my cheeks, I decided that one day when I grew up I would help as many kids as I could in honor of my little sister.

It's hard for our natural mind to comprehend God's love. He transcends a government structure, an earthly impossibility, and human pain. That childhood experience continually reminds me of God's ability to reveal Himself to us, to show us His love, to silence the voice of despair within our hearts. We just have to look outside of ourselves long enough and we will see Him.

A year passed, and my dad and mom decided to adopt a little boy from the local orphanage. Another painful heartache made its way through the doors of our home. We were denied the adoption because we were too poor to take care of him. And there I was again. This time it was a clear summer night. Standing on the balcony, I once again looked into the sky and made another decision. I wanted to help as many orphaned boys and girls as I possibly could in honor of this little orphaned child whom I never had the opportunity to meet.

Another defining moment.
Another invisible mentor.
Another redeemed memory.

An experience that could have remained dreadful, filling me with regret and unforgiveness, was instead redeemed by giving it a purpose and focusing on a future bigger than pain or death. A future of helping someone else.

Within the first year of my arrival and studies in Tulsa, Oklahoma, I began to support a child from an orphanage in Bulgaria with $1 per month. It wasn't much. But it was all I had, and it was only the start. Today our organization has helped hundreds of children, not only in Bulgaria, but in Africa and other parts of the world. I have traveled extensively, speaking and raising money for those who have no voice to speak for themselves, because I chose to travel the stairway of my past memories and bring them with me into my future. They give me the greatest purpose—to live beyond my pain, to help those who get stuck on the wrong stairways of life and to lead them through the transforming desert to a place of safety that only God provides.

Naomi and Ruth, the past and the future, were safely embraced in the Promised Land. I particularly love the conclusion of this story. Boaz, a close relative of Elimelech, later became the kinsman-redeemer. A wealthy and respected man, he chose to marry Ruth and purchase the land that belonged to Naomi. By doing so, the land remained in the family and Naomi could live without debt or shame. Her past was forgiven. At the same time, Ruth's future was redeemed, and she could continue to live in the Promised Land.

Boaz as a representation of Christ reveals God's willingness to meet us in our strengths and in our weaknesses. Jesus is our ultimate Redeemer, the One who paid the debt for our past mistakes and who is able to infuse our memories with purpose, to qualify us to live a life of dignity. His presence will empower you with strength and courage to travel the stairs of your memories and find renewed hope and victory.

AN EXPERIENTIAL IMAGERY EXERCISE

You may color and write on the stairs. Using one or two words, describe significant memories that have given your life greater purpose and helped you overcome problems or challenges. You can place them chronologically starting at the top of the stairway.

PRINCIPLE

Memories are like stairs—they lead you forward when you utilize them as a bridge between your past and your future. Depending on how you perceive them, they can empower you or defeat you. When memories are given purpose and destination, they can help you overcome any challenge in life.

Take time to think through the process, using it as a stairway to bridge your past and your future. *The goal is to learn how to reflect upon and reinstate the feelings from your accomplishments and victories, so you can have greater confidence when faced with new challenges.*

What strengths have you developed during your journey of walking through these challenges? List 5–10 strengths.

-
-
-
-
-

-
-
-
-
-

What have you learned during or after the journey?

What positive feelings emerge from your memories of overcoming the challenges you have faced?

-

-

-

-

-

How can you implement the strengths and feelings of victory from the past in a current situation you are facing?

WHEN YOUR DREAMS TAKE FLIGHT

LEARN HOW TO MANAGE YOUR BRIEFCASE

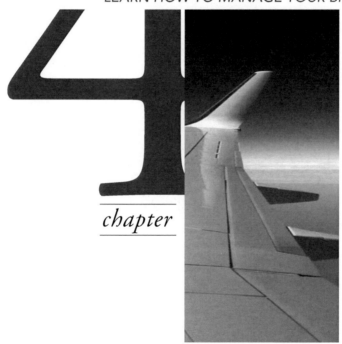

chapter

I dream my painting and I paint my dream."[1]

– VINCENT VAN GOGH

"ARE YOU READY? WE CAN'T BE LATE!"

Filled with joy and anticipation, my dad's voice echoed down the hallway. With a radiant glow, my mom followed close behind.

10 years of waiting patiently.

10 years of preparing expectantly.

10 years of saving diligently.

My dad's ticket number was next on the list. He was called in to pay for the purchase of his long-awaited dream car—a brand-new red Russian Lada! Leaning over the balcony railing, I blew them a kiss and awaited their return. News about the car quickly spread through the neighborhood. By the time my parents returned home with their prize, all the neighbors and most of our relatives were at our house, eagerly waiting to see and touch the wonder.

---

[1] "Vincent Van Gogh," Goodreads.com.

Purchasing a vehicle under communism was anything but simple. You couldn't just go to a car dealership whenever you wanted to and buy one. Everything was regulated, including

> your needs,
>> your wants,
>>> your dreams.

Everyone was required to follow a certain process. First, you had to place a 3,000 Leva[2] deposit to hold your spot on the waiting list. That in itself was a lifetime of savings, and there was no guarantee that you would ever see your investment pay off. Second, you indicated the model, year, and color of the car you desired. The choices were restricted based on import. Third, you were given a number handwritten on a piece of paper, which must be preserved until you received notification to pick up the car. Since import from the Soviet Union was extremely limited and hundreds of people were on that waiting list, it took ten to fifteen years before your "life-changing" opportunity arrived. Then, once you received the call, you had to be prepared to pay for your car in cash. If you did not have the money or were not able to get to the dealership when specified, your number was placed back on the waiting list for an uncertain number of years.

Looking back, I am in awe of the patience we all developed during these waiting periods. A desire to achieve or hold on to a dream can wither and die if suppressed for a long period of time without any tangible visibility. Despite the fact that the choices were limited and my dad was only allowed to dream within certain parameters, he never wavered from the hope given to him. Each month, he set aside money from his paycheck for the car. Sometimes he would pull out the number to reassure himself that it was real, and other times he would share his dreams with me of the day he would drive all of us to the Black Sea for vacation. The vision of the car was so real in his mind that it gave him hope and discipline during the waiting period.

Though external circumstances such as cultural or family environments can restrict the size of a dream, no one can stop you from dreaming. It's part of our human nature. The difference, however, is in the activation and realization of the dream. It's not enough to just have a dream in your mind. If it only remains internal, it is an easy target for

> disappointment,
>> condemnation,
>>> cynical unbelief.

---

[2] Leva is the Bulgarian currency. As of February 2017, 3,000 Leva equals about $1,650 USD. In the early '80s, the average monthly salary was about 200–250 Leva.

The true parameters for the achievement of a dream come from a place and purpose beyond ourselves.

A dream is...

ignited within our imagination,
aligned with the desires of our hearts,
fueled by our passion,
carried out by our will.

When a dream comes from a purpose greater than ourselves,
it will always generate the stamina needed
to launch.
It will love flexibility over routine,
longevity over short-term gratification,
and it will have lasting impact.

Our vision gives our dream *perspective*.
Our focus gives our dream a *destination*.
Our purpose gives our dream an *engine*.
Our goals give our dream a *departure time*.
Our desires give our dream a *runway*.
Our experiences give our dream *wings*.
Our potential gives our dream *altitude*.

How Your Dreams Develop Wings

When God asked Abram to leave the land of Ur, He gave him a promise that through his offspring he would become a father of many nations. God did something important in expanding Abram's vision, which we read about in Genesis 15:5: "Then He brought him outside and said, 'Look now toward heaven, and count the stars if you are able to number them.' And He said to him, 'So shall your descendants be.'"

First Abram had to go out of his own land and comfort zone. Second, he had to look outside of himself, into the greatness of God. Third, he had to see. Fourth, he had to count. His internal image needed to catch up with the powerful image of God's external dream for him. However, Abram did what most of us would have done: he brought the supernatural vision down to a natural level of accomplishment. When he looked up to see the stars, his external view changed, but his internal comfort zone remained the same. So, he began to fulfill a dream based solely on his own understanding.

God didn't put a number on Abram's dream. He only asked him to count. Oftentimes, instead of "counting" the possibilities God has for us, we become discouraged and tell ourselves, "That's bigger than me; I am not sure if it's possible" or "That should be enough. It's bigger than what anyone else I know has done." As long as we remain in our current comfort zone of possibilities, our dreams are confined within the walls of our natural mind-set.

Because she was barren, Abram's wife Sarai advised him to take her maid Hagar as a second wife so she could conceive a child. Ishmael was born out of impatience, within the comfort zone of Abram and Sarai in their limited perception of God's promise. Whenever we achieve something based on our own ability, it will remain dependent on us for its life. It will also pull us back to our old habits and attitudes, constantly reminding us of the person we know ourselves to be. When our current comfort zone does not expand to match the size of our dream, we will overachieve in areas already familiar to us and create justifying reasons against flexibility and change.

Gestalt psychology[3] supports this theory. It suggests that human beings are always working to create order in their minds—matching the picture of how they view the outside world with their current view of reality. When the picture of our future dream does not match our perception with the present reality of our life, anxiety, stress, and tension increase. Often we don't know how to reconcile the discrepancy between the present and the future in our minds, therefore we return to our accustomed comfort zone.

When God called Abram "a father of many nations" and changed his name to Abraham in Genesis 17:4–5, it didn't mean that Abraham began to automatically function in this new vision. In fact, he laughed at the thought that he and Sarai (now named Sarah) could possibly have their own child. Our old mind-set will always try to justify the *how* in the fulfillment of a dream that is bigger than us. Most people stop at "How is this going to come to pass?" because they cannot see the supernatural from a natural comfort zone. Just because Abraham *saw*, he didn't automatically *become*. Seeing a dream and seeing ourselves at the achievement level of that dream are not the same thing. The longer we look at a dream without expanding our internal comfort zone, the more it will appear as a threat. Eventually, we will abandon it rather than look for ways to achieve it.

---

[3] For more information on Gestalt psychology, see Gary Yontef, Gestalt.org/yontef.htm.

In order for your dream to have wings and take flight, you first need an awareness of your starting point. Where are you presently? What is your current reality? Who makes up your reality? Is it you? Is it God's Word? Or is it the culture, the social media, the opinions of others? For Abraham and Sarah, the reality was their age: they were too old to conceive and have a son. That reality was no obstacle to God, who transcends our human characteristics and abilities, but it caused them to remain in their human comfort zone, closing their minds from seeing God's supernatural power at work.

Neuroscience offers an explanation for the dream-turned-threat phenomenon. From the base of our brain to the central cortex, a network of cells form our reticular activating system (RAS).[4] Its job is to help us sort through information and keep us focused. Based on what we perceive as a value or as a threat, our RAS will automatically refocus our attention. It works on two levels: in order to assimilate the importance of the information, the person providing it must be of value to us. If the person is not of value to us, we will dismiss the information, even if it is valuable. The opposite is also true: if the person is of no value to us, but they share information that is a threat to us, we automatically will pay attention to the information, because now the threat exceeds the value.

Likewise, when we perceive our dreams to be greater than our ability to execute them, our RAS will interpret them as a threat, which in turn will cause us to run away and dismiss the value of God's ability to bring them to pass. If we direct our RAS to always look for the threat in the impossibility, we will stay stuck in life, unable to see the correct value or possible ways of achievement. Most of our dreams die because we failed to understand how to change our internal comfort zone to match our external vision, not because we didn't start off with great ambitions.

ENABLING YOUR DREAMS TO SOAR

During my first year of studies in Tulsa, I was asked what I would *not* want to be doing five years after graduation. In large letters I wrote in my journal: "I do not want to sit by the window dreaming of what my life could look like one day. I want to be actively involved in the dream of my life."

A dream needs to be consistently infused with knowledge obtained from our relationship with God and life's lessons. In order for us to have a peaceful coexistence between our dreams and our mind-set, we must give our RAS freedom to seek the *how* by clearly defining the end result of our goal. In general, typical goal-setting involves a written

---

[4] Tice and Quick, *Personal Coaching for Results,* 94–96.

plan of action steps. They are necessary to have, but should not be set as the only directive toward achieving our desired results.

Often during our team planning meetings, Lou Tice would use the phrase *free-flow goal setting*. He encouraged us not to get stuck in a natural mind-set of setting goals but rather to ask God's guidance and allow our RAS to find the answers. The best ideas are often a thought away, but when we force our mind to find the solution, our train of thought slows down, even to the point of standstill. The moment we establish our plan as the final goal, we stop our RAS from seeing other possibilities outside the limits of our list.

Since we are created in the image of God, we are created to dream as He does, without limits or boundaries. It all begins with imagination. The more we dwell upon, think about, and imagine something, the more precisely we will begin to understand it. The greater the clarity,
> the more detail we can see.
>> The greater the detail,
>>> the more options we discover
>>>> in bringing a dream to pass.

The Gospel of John 3:1–21 gives us a reference to the term "born again," used by Jesus during a conversation He had with Nicodemus, a prominent Pharisee and member of the Sanhedrin. It actually means to be born from above and refers to God's eternal life imparted to those who believe in Christ. When we enter into a personal relationship with Christ, we receive guidance and direction in our daily affairs through the Holy Spirit. Our spirit, soul, and body become redeemed and are no longer under the control of our old nature or our old comfort zone of living.[5]

In other words, our mind, with our RAS, is now under the influence of the Holy Spirit. When we begin to think about godly things—what is positive and edifying, lovely and praiseworthy—our RAS will begin to see and lead us to places, people, and opportunities we may not have seen before because our value system has changed. Through our redemption, we have transitioned from seeing in fear to envisioning with the eyes of faith. What we used to perceive as a threat, we can now recognize as valuable. Once our eyes are opened to God's Kingdom principles and His plans for us, our mind becomes our greatest asset in attaining our dreams, not solely based on our natural instincts but on the daily leading of God's Spirit. Creativity and sustained energy will be released from within us until we see our dreams take flight.

---

[5] 1 John 5:1–2, Colossians 3:1–4, Philippians 4:8–9.

We become like that upon which we focus. We adopt the direction of the path that is dominant in our thoughts. If our mind is always focused on "This can't happen," "I am not good enough," "I don't have the money and connections I need," then we suppress our potential and minimize our abilities. The clearer your vision, the more your mind will subconsciously adjust in that direction. All of a sudden, instead of just looking at God's promises and plans, you will see yourself in them.

While it is important to surround yourself with people to encourage you and remind you of the direction you want to go, you must also build the internal strength to sustain yourself even when you do not have that support. This happens when the urgency of the fulfillment of your dream places a demand for growth and expansion beyond your present comfort zone. When you are no longer satisfied with your current reality, the necessity to change will become internally driven. You develop a path of personal accountability. No one will have to motivate you to become more disciplined. Your inner need to fully live your dream will outgrow any excuses, fears, and doubts you have had.

KISS YOUR DREAMS AT NIGHT

During my first two years of college, I lived with three roommates. Sleeping on the top bunk bed, I was so close to the ceiling I could touch it. Prior to falling asleep, my mind was actively involved in bringing my dreams into reality. I purposefully read about God's miracles, which fueled my desire to preach and minister around the world, to meet with presidents and prominent dignitaries, and to influence nations. As I studied biographies of people who had made a vast impact around the world, I cut out pictures and articles. Sometimes I put them up on the ceiling so I could look at the images at night. I literally could kiss the pictures on my ceiling. When you "kiss" your dream, you begin to speak your future into your present.

Gradually, my internal view of myself became much more defined, and even my outward appearance began to change.

My steps became more confident.

My eyes had a new spark.

My face had a hopeful glow.

On my way to classes, I would confidently carry the small green plastic briefcase I had brought from Bulgaria. As I walked, I imagined myself speaking in front of thousands of people or meeting dignitaries. It didn't matter whether people ignored me or didn't believe me; my internal vision carried greater power than their view of me.

One day in Dallas, Texas, while waiting for the flight that would take me to my very first speaking engagement, someone asked me what I did for a living. I was twenty-one at the time. Boldly raising my green plastic briefcase, I replied, "I am an ambassador to the nations. I deliver good news when I meet with presidents. I help them change policies and believe in God."

The person practically laughed in my face and said, "Yeah, right! You must have lost your mind!"

To which I thought, *Yes, I did lose my natural mind-set, because I see it by faith. I know it will come to pass.*

If you need other people's approval of your ability to achieve your dream, then you are still living in a state of admiring the dream, rather than being fully immersed in it. In the beginning it will be important to carry your dream hidden in the "briefcase" of your imagination until it becomes vivid enough to alter the neurons of your brain. Once your mind-set is switched, no one can stop you! You will fearlessly live out the reality of what you imagined, silencing the voices of the skeptics.

The dream God gave Abraham encompassed a world much larger than him and Sarah. God is known to deposit in us seeds of faith and of dreams that are meant to reach more than one person. Many people have great ambitions for fame, but these are not necessarily the dreamers that go down in history as world-changers.

On August 28, 1963, Martin Luther King, Jr. delivered his legendary "I Have a Dream" speech before 250,000 people in Washington, DC. How could so many people have gathered without any social media advertisement at that time? People came for themselves, because his dream carried the familiar voice of their own dream. Dr. King shared what he *believed*—a dream, not a plan—and that belief resonated in hearts as they took up the cause as their own, spread the word, and gathered in solidarity around that common dream.[6]

LIVING FOR SIGNIFICANCE

Many men and women of the Bible, whose names are not often mentioned, made vast historical shifts in their society. Such a person is a woman by the name of Huldah. Mentioned briefly in 2 Kings 22 and 2 Chronicles 34, she lived in Jerusalem under King Josiah. She was a prophetess through whom the entire nation moved from idol worship to remembering their true God. Huldah not only interpreted the meaning of the Book of the Law, but with boldness she prophesied what was to come. Because of

---

[6] Sinek, "How great leaders inspire action," YouTube Video.

the preparation of one woman, King Josiah heard, listened, and obeyed the word forth. Under his reign, Judah prospered as God was worshiped and glorified once again.

When we shift our vision from *me* to *we* and focus on helping others, our dreams begin to carry a deeper purpose. Sometimes God will ask us to take the lead or to empower other people's dreams. Other times, He will use us to direct the dreamers to a place of restoration and refuge.

Perhaps you don't have ambitions to change the whole world, but you do have a dream to see your family succeed or your friends and coworkers live a better life. Maybe you can be a part of helping others through hidden tasks such as prayer, giving, acts of kindness, and obedience to what God is asking you to do in a particular season in life. Most likely your dream is different from mine, but the question to ask is, "Am I living in a state of constant preparation or in a state of mindless stagnation?" If your dreams remain superficial you will miss many opportunities due to lack of preparation.

Chances are, people like Huldah didn't wake up in the morning thinking one day they would be part of a great Bible story.

But they woke up!

And every day they were alive in their dream,

doing their part.

I know of a man by the name of Dobri Dobrev, usually referred to as "Grandpa" Dobri, or "Diado" Dobri in Bulgarian. Born in 1914, he spent years of his life begging outside the Orthodox cathedral in Sofia, Bulgaria. His long white beard, chiseled features, and shabby appearance were a familiar sight to passersby. A few years ago, his compassionate deeds

"Grandpa" Dobri
The Silent Angel – The True Story of Dobri Dobrev

were discovered. The money he had obtained by begging on the streets had all been given to local orphanages and to help with the restoration of historical monasteries and churches. Close to 40,000 euros were dispensed through this man who in the eyes of society was a worthless beggar.

The news of "Grandpa" Dobri traveled quickly over social media and people came from all over the world to meet with him. Documentaries depicted his life and deeds, and he became revered by many as a saint. When one interviewer asked him why he did what he did, his response was, "We must love each other as God loves us."[7]

While some strive to achieve a successful career through their dreams and visions, people like Dobri Dobrev adopt the needs of others as their own. When we do that, our dream to help outgrows our natural environment. We move from living for success to living for significance when we no longer care if people validate our achievements. Significance is not about our earthly reputation but about a lasting and eternal impact on individuals and society.

When Your Dream Is the New Normal

One moment in time can make a vast impact on generations to come. On June 12, 1987, segments of news coverage from the Brandenburg Gate in Berlin, Germany, brought a message of hope. As family and friends squeezed next to our 15-inch black-and-white TV screen in the kitchen, intently reading tiny subtitles, the penetrating voice of U.S. President Ronald Reagan spoke compelling words of freedom. *There is something different in the voice of this man,* I thought. He spoke
    with conviction,
        with passion,
            with boldness.

"General Secretary Gorbachev, if you seek peace, if you seek prosperity for the Soviet Union and Eastern Europe, if you seek liberalization, come here to this gate. Mr. Gorbachev, open this gate. Mr. Gorbachev, tear down this wall!"

He continued, "As I looked out a moment ago from the Reichstag, that embodiment of German unity, I noticed words crudely spray-painted upon the wall, perhaps by a young Berliner: 'This wall will fall. Beliefs become reality.' Yes, across Europe, this wall will fall. For it cannot withstand faith; it cannot withstand truth. The wall cannot withstand freedom."[8]

Did someone just shatter the false reality of our lives? For many years we had been taught that America was our biggest enemy. Yet somehow this voice made its way through the cracks of our distorted existence. It stirred curiosity. It ignited hope. His words shone a light on the hidden path to our freedom. We gazed at each other, speechless, as if slowly

---

[7] Dobrev, *Mite*, Pokrov Foundation, YouTube Video.
[8] ReaganFoundation, "Berlin Wall," YouTube Video.

awakening from a nightmare, once again sensing…hoping…*knowing* that change was on the horizon. The days of the sleeping giant were numbered.

Liberation had put its foot in the crack of the doorway and began to split across the European territory. Two short years later, on November 9, 1989, the gates of the Berlin Wall were opened and people from East and West Germany united under the sign of freedom. Families separated for decades were joyfully reunited. A new uprising of the human spirit emerged from beneath the cold bricks of the Wall.

Revolutionary freedom swept through Poland and Hungary with a domino effect and twenty-four hours later knocked on the doors of Bulgaria. On November 10, the Bulgarian president Todor Zhivkov announced his "retirement" after 35 years of dictatorship.[9]

> People of all ages packed the streets.
> > Sounds of celebration
> > > mixed with restrained chaos.

"Freedom! Freedom! No more communism!" The voices rang through the night and for years to come.

As I look in retrospect on President Reagan's speech,
> one day,
> > one person,
> > > one action,

marked the beginning of liberation and the end of the Cold War era. By the end of 1990, the Berlin Wall was torn down altogether with the collapse of communism throughout the rest of Eastern Europe and in Soviet Russia itself.

To this day, my heart remains stirred with even greater emotion and deeper appreciation for the freedom of human rights and dignity—independence we all must protect and liberty we must fight for with fortitude.

Curiously, the same speech that birthed optimism in us was criticized as not having much impact on the decision to tear down the Wall, let alone an impact on the people he addressed. Even within his own administration, President Reagan's words were considered a source of controversy. What was a dream for liberation in one man's heart was perceived as a threat by those about to lose their power. When dreams born through purpose are planted with the seed of nonconformity, they will carry the

---

[9] Though Bulgaria was under the dictatorship style of Todor Zhivkov and the Communist Party for 35 years, the actual rule of the Party lasted almost 45 years.

power to withstand opposition;
power to withstand judgment;
power to withstand manipulation.

The voices of naysayers will be drowned out by the testimonies of those whose lives have been positively affected. While history can be altered and facts can be erased, the truth will always be judged in the courtroom of the human heart. When lives have been changed for the better, then the purpose of the dream has been achieved.

Some dreams only live to liberate one generation, but their impact is carried throughout history as they inspire bravery in the next. No one can determine all that encompasses. Just like Abraham couldn't count the stars, we will not be able to count the lives affected until we are on the other side of this earthly life. The generations ahead of us will be the recipients of the dreams we have said *yes* to, the dreams that were bigger than us.

On May 16, 2012, at 6:30 p.m., on the fifth floor of The Pacific Institute in Seattle, another transformational event took place in my life.
Cameras all around,
eyes looking up,
ears intently absorbing
the speech given by one man.

This time I was not watching on a small black-and-white TV; I was present among dignitaries and world leaders listening to the first democratic President of Bulgaria, Rosen Plevneliev. Through a series of opportunities, I found myself as a lead organizer hosting him and his Cabinet during his first presidential visit to the United States. His

Bulgarian President Plevneliev shares an inspiring message at The Pacific Institute.

With President Plevneliev during the Seattle event.

closing remarks drew enthusiastic applause as he declared, "The determination of the Bulgarian spirit to fight for freedom cannot be quenched."

I shared the same conviction. Filled with a storm of emotions I am unable to describe here, I felt that day marked the continuation of the fulfillment of what God had spoken to me and the beginning of the liberation process my ministry team and I were committed to bring forth in my nation.

Your invisible mentors speak the most profoundly in your life when no one is watching—in the silence when no one but you and God hear the voices of fear threatening to kill your dream. And yet, you still hold on,
> willing to believe a revelation,
> > willing to arise because of dedication, and
> > > willing to accept the dream.

Integration is not only important during the dreaming stage, but also when we begin to see our dreams come to pass. One afternoon, after hosting some influential delegates in Seattle, Lou Tice asked me what I thought about the meetings.

"Wow! This was amazing!" I responded.

He quickly corrected me, "Don't use 'this was' when you achieve a segment of your dream. If you view your accomplishment only in past tense, it will always remain there without the opportunity to change the construct of your mind. With each new achievement tell yourself, 'This is my new normal.' Then you can safely adopt your present realization of the achievement to attain future goals."

In psychological terms, the neural firing after the achievement of a goal produces proteins that assist with the fusing of the activated neurons. In their book *The Whole-Brain Child*, Dr. Daniel Siegel and Dr. Tina Bryson state:

> *Neurons that fire together wire together. This entire process—from neural activation to neural growth and strengthened connections—is neuroplasticity. Essentially, it means that the brain itself is plastic or changing, based on what we experience, and what we give our attention to.... This is how practice can become a skill and how a state can become a trait, for good or for bad.* [10]

In other words, when you embrace your achievement as your new normal, the neurons of your brain "glue" it together. Now you not only have a redeemed memory (as we

---

[10] Siegel and Bryson, *The Whole-Brain Child*, 99.

discussed in Chapter 3), but you have safely transitioned your new accomplishment from an external experience to a cohesive integration in your mind-set. Then you can confidently and humbly continue to walk toward new horizons of freedom.

AN EXPERIENTIAL IMAGERY EXERCISE

You may color or write inside the empty picture frames. In each frame, use specific words to describe your dream(s). As you read and look over your dream board on this graphic, allow your imagination to fill in the details in the pictures.

Suggestion: *Besides the graphic in this book, you may want to utilize additional creative methods and online resources—apps, photos, articles, etc.—to make your dream board colorful and clear. When you are able to see yourself as part of your dreams, your thoughts will free-flow into seeing new opportunities on how to fulfill them.*

PRINCIPLE

Dreams must be given wings through your imagination so they can fly. They must be given purpose so they can develop. When you see yourself in your dream through proper integration of your achievements, you will have a sustained energy to reach your destination.

Take the time to think about your dreams. *Some dreams will come to pass sooner than others; some will take a lifetime to achieve, and with others you will only plant a seed for the next generation to carry forth.*

Categorize your dreams in outline form within this section or on a separate piece of paper. *For example, Personal, Family, Business, Vacation, Health, Travel, Finances, Ministry, Noble Projects, etc. How far along are you in the process of their achievement? Next to each dream, place your starting date and rate your progress (0–10). Use this list as a reference point to monitor your progress.*

Who has affected your life in a positive way? What have you learned from those people? Next to their names write down the qualities you admire, the work they have done, the impact they have made in your personal life and/or the world.

Which of the qualities exemplified by these people could you adopt into your life to help you move toward the realization of your dream(s)?

SKYDIVING WITH A 12,000-FOOT PERSPECTIVE
KEEP YOUR MOUTH CLOSED AND LISTEN TO THE LANDING INSTRUCTIONS

chapter

When you reach the end of your rope, tie a knot in it and **hang on.**"[1]

– PROVERB FROM THE AMERICAN WEST

PIERCING WIND cut through my jumpsuit into my bones. I couldn't slow my rapid descent toward the sandy soil any more than I could grab onto the clouds around me for stability. Gravity ruled. Worse, the view of the landing strip became more elusive as my disorientation increased. Finally accepting that I had no control over the next twenty minutes of the unknown, I stopped fighting. My only safety was in trusting my guide and letting go.

Daringly.

Unreservedly.

Completely.

---

[1] Pearce, "The English Proverb in New Mexico," *California Folklore Quarterly.*

While I had flown on many planes before, that day marked my first 12,000-foot skydive through the friendly skies. Fortunately, I was not alone. Safely resting in the knowledge of my instructor's professional abilities (and the harness that connected us!), I drew strength from his calm instructions.

"Relax. Pull your body horizontally and bend your legs. Stretch your arms forward and wave at the camera," he told me.

The cameraman had jumped fifteen seconds ahead of us, recording my every move. *I better make sure and look good for the camera, 'cause I am not planning on making this a lifestyle!* I thought. The wind was winning over my smiling expressions, abruptly stretching and moving the skin on my face.

High adventure!

Somehow I managed to yell, "I love it! This is so fun!" As I waved at the camera, sudden, intrusive thoughts tried to steal my new feeling of accomplishment. *Who am I kidding? This is nothing like what I imagined!*

"When are we landing?" I asked in a panic.

"Landing? We just started," my instructor replied. "Soon we'll be gliding. You'll like that! But you must let your body stay in a relaxed position in order to enjoy the full experience."

The harness hugged me tightly, and I could feel my breath slowly escape my body. I was still trying to smile for the camera while my saliva was getting sucked out by the speed of the descent, splashing all over my face.

"Keep your mouth shut and breathe through your nose!" Both the cameraman and my instructor were shouting over the noise of the wind.

In a matter of seconds, we had reached 5,000 feet, where I was to release the parachute handle. Caught up in the action, I completely forgot. Fortunately, my instructor didn't fail to save us both. We felt the sudden jolt as the parachute billowed open, jerking us back up into the clouds. We slowed significantly. Loosening my harness helped my breathing and normalized my heartbeat. Finally, we were gliding.

A picturesque view caught my attention. The setting sun covered the ocean with a translucent glow of golden rays, and the sky appeared as though dipped in brilliant nuances of pink, coral, and scarlet. Majestic mountains topped with snow peeked through the puffy clouds. These thrilling moments of scenic beauty made the fear and emotional roller coaster of the jump worth it all.

We continued to circle in the air until I became comfortable with the landing process. Cheered by those who had jumped ahead of us, we finally approached solid ground. Somehow I managed to raise my legs high enough and then run simultaneously with my instructor down the landing strip.

"Wave and smile at the video camera," he reminded me. Safe landing—it was time to celebrate!

SEEING BEYOND THE HORIZON OF IMMEDIATE ACHIEVEMENT

Similar to my skydiving adventure, most of us jump into thin air without a clear vision of what comes next.
> Old fears get stirred within us
> > creating memory deficiencies,
> > > stealing the breath from our ideas,
> > > > leaving us embarrassed in front of the camera
> > > > > meant to record our success.

Impatiently, we seek the landing strip where big aspirations entice us with their glamour. But the competitive rat race of our social environment stirs a false sense of urgency in us. Rather than simply savoring the pleasant experience of gliding, our reckless impatience to land pressures us to forfeit the process and reach our destination prematurely.

I learned an important lesson that afternoon: being prepared for the landing and having a precise mental picture of it is as imperative as the initial jump. During the gliding time, while hidden in the clouds, I received my landing instructions. I was directed on how far to bend my knees and lift my legs upon descent. At that point the harness would take on my weight and pull me back toward the instructor so he could direct the parachute. In addition, I had to promise that I would allow him to place his feet on the ground first to prevent any harm to either of us or to others at the landing strip.

In the same way, we may often disconnect God's security harness and accept the illusion of freedom. The thrill of speed, though lasting only a moment, lures us. Perhaps for years we have been flying through life without proper attachment to God, misconstruing the speed of gravity as achieved independence.

Our instinct is to try to control what we fear or what we lack knowledge to properly handle. Our minds continually look for what comes next. When we don't have a new immediate focus, our stress level increases. In order to grow into our potential, we must aim beyond the initial skydive toward the dream and allow sufficient time for learning, planning, releasing, and landing. This is called forethought—a preparation process crucial for moving through our first achievement and on to the next.

How we process the period in between the completion of one goal and the start of another is key to not losing momentum, mentally and emotionally. The excitement of the event—anticipation and exhilaration, the pressure and the challenge—releases an addictive adrenaline rush, but after the objective is attained, the rush is over. That can create an emotional letdown or a return to safety in our routine.

This is a normal bodily response to an intense experience. But if not recognized accurately, it can lead to loss of energy and alertness, emotional and physical depletion, depression, and suicidal thoughts. It's not far from the truth to say that most people *die* before their death. Their dreams, desires, and visions perish within them because their earthly lives suffered a certain form of devastation, and they were unable to recover from it. Sometimes we call it burnout, other times, hopeless existence. It could also be said that the transition after the dream lacked adequate forethought and planning.

To take a break after a major accomplishment is important. When we give ourselves permission to stop and recharge after an achievement, we will subconsciously adjust to enjoy the time of rest. Failing to choose to do so will cause us to become restless, and out of guilt—believing that we should keep busy—we will try to outdo a previous accomplishment. If you make an intentional decision to rest, you will have the ability to enjoy your downtime—or, in skydiving terms, your gliding time. Then you can joyfully enter your next season with peace and assurance.

FINDING OUR "NEXT"

Pilots can become disoriented during flight if they do not have clear visibility. The external conditions will confuse their interpretation of what they see. On July 16, 1999, John F. Kennedy Jr. died in a plane crash in the Atlantic off the coast of Massachusetts. Later, authorities discovered that he was certified to fly only under visual flight rules (VFR). Pilots rely on the general weather conditions under VFR.

Clear visual orientation in relation to the ground helps them steer the aircraft and keep from crashing into other objects. If the weather is foggy, with low visibility, the pilot must use instrumental flight rules (IFR) to navigate in spite of not being able to see the relation to the ground.

Unfortunately, the weather and light conditions were not favorable that night. The National Transportation Safety Board based Kennedy's crash on spatial disorientation[2]—a pilot having a false or confused sense of direction.

When we lose our focus and our vision is clouded, our external environment will seem to hinder us rather than help us develop in life. In order to avoid "spatial disorientation," we must become educated about the dangers life presents us. God is our instructor and His Word establishes secure boundaries for our lives, giving us the instrumental flight rules for landing at our future destination. However, our personal applications and experiences of God's Word often depend on our perception. We must compare our perceptions with the contextual alignment of Scripture to ensure an accurate interpretation of His Word. Otherwise, deceptive beliefs will sneak in and send us on a trajectory that results in self-sabotaging actions.

One of the most significant prophets in the Old Testament was Elijah, remembered for his faithfulness to God and an extraordinary life of wonders and fulfillment of God's promises for humanity. Yet while he experienced the heights of greatness and supernatural miracles, he also felt the depths of despair, disorientation, and doubt.

After more than three years of devastating drought, Israel had turned again to false gods. In order to see his people return to the true living God, Elijah challenged evil King Ahab to a showdown on Mount Carmel. In a dramatic scene, the Israelites gathered with the 450 prophets of Baal and the 400 prophets of Asherah to see which god would send down fire from heaven to consume the sacrifice.

For hours, the false prophets wailed, mutilated themselves, and prayed to their gods, but the only response was silence. Elijah called the Israelites together, rebuilt the broken altar, and prepared the sacrifice. Then he cried out to God with unwavering faith and boldness:

> "LORD *God of Abraham, Isaac, and Israel, let it be known this day that You are God in Israel and I am Your servant, and that I have done all these things at Your word. Hear me, O LORD, hear me, that this people may know that You are the*

---

[2] NTSB, July 6, 2000, ntsb.gov/news/2000.

LORD God, and that You have turned their hearts back to You again." (1 Kings 18:36–37).

And the Lord responded with power and authority.

The fire from heaven fell.

The sacrifice was consumed.

The children of Israel returned to their God.

The miracle was completed.

Could there be anything greater for

Elijah's "next"?

Sudden fear took over Elijah. His enemy sent forth a word declaring his death and destruction, and the news consumed his soul like the flames that had devoured the sacrifice. Elijah fled to Beersheba, where he prayed that he might die. His trust in God had unconsciously come to an end. An angel brought him food and water, and Elijah journeyed for forty days to Horeb, the mountain of God, where he hid in a cave. He had bought into the lie that he was the only prophet left, doomed to die by the wrath of Jezebel, wife of King Ahab. Dismissing the greatness of God, he disconnected himself from the "harness" and plunged full speed into the spiral of his soul's despair.

When we experience an emotional high after God has used our gifts or talents, we may resort to seeking validation from others in order to sustain the positive feelings of our mountaintop event. We must take time to process the experience and, through our forethought, implement the lessons learned. Otherwise, the mountaintop success can easily destroy us when our character does not match our actions. Character and self-assurance are best developed during our alone times with God, when we are hidden away—gliding. Then His power is released to flow out of us as we approach the landing strip of ministry, business, and other opportunities. People often desire to live on the landing strip or in front of the camera when they first begin. But true moments of victory are always won in life's invisible intervals, *before* a fire from Heaven can be released into the visible realms.

So often, we want to be remembered as superheroes, reluctant to reveal the times when we are inadequate and failing, feeling sorry for ourselves, doubting God or our own faith in Him. We must remember that when miracles happen and place us on the mountaintop of life, they are not a reflection of our level of faith. Miracles reveal God's ability to back up His Word in and through us, so that He will be glorified during the process. However, if we mistake the manifestation of the miracle as a stamp of approval (or the lack of miracles as a stamp of disapproval) on our faith in Christ, then we are playing God. If we take the navigation of the parachute in our own hands, the moment we are hidden in the clouds we will equate it as a season of loss rather than a repositioning, a new elevation of perspective and empowerment to better achieve what God has for us next.

Elijah's "next" consisted of hiding and giving up, while God had a different vision for him. All was not lost. In Elijah's cave of despair, the Lord chose to speak to him. Not through the wind, not through the earthquake, and not through the fire, but in a gentle whisper. And Elijah heard His voice. 1 Kings 19:13–18 portrays a powerful development in the story:

> So it was, when Elijah heard it, that he wrapped his face in his mantle and went out and stood in the entrance of the cave. Suddenly a voice came to him, and said, "What are you doing here, Elijah?" And he said, "I have been very zealous for the LORD God of hosts; because the children of Israel have forsaken Your covenant, torn down Your altars, and killed Your prophets with the sword. I alone am left; and they seek to take my life."

> Then the LORD said to him: "Go, return on your way to the Wilderness of Damascus; and when you arrive, anoint Hazael as king over Syria. Also you shall anoint Jehu the son of Nimshi as king over Israel. And Elisha the son of Shaphat of Abel Meholah you shall anoint as prophet in your place.... Yet I have reserved seven thousand in Israel, all whose knees have not bowed to Baal, and every mouth that has not kissed him."

In verses 9 and 13 of 1 Kings 19, God asks Elijah the same question: "What are you doing here?" And both times, Elijah responds, "I alone am left; and they seek to take my life." It's as though he had rehearsed his speech in his mind. Isn't that what we often do? Our mind goes on autopilot because when we are overwhelmed our peace leaves and so does our ability to properly discern. Once we lock on to fear, we cannot find the solution.

Our minds are not designed to see two pictures simultaneously. Even if we are trying hard to look at a double image on a picture, we will only see one or the other at a time. The same applies to real life. When we compare the impossibility next to God, we either assimilate it as a problem or we see God's greatness to solve it. But to try to focus simultaneously on both creates confusion in our mind and leads to distortion of our vision and faith.

We must keep in perspective that when God asks us a question, He looks for an answer not because He doesn't know, but for us to hear our own beliefs, convictions, and fears.

Only when we allow ourselves to hear

what our soul is crying for,

expressed out loud—

only then we can begin to

look for an answer.

Then our eyes are opened again to see. Then we have given our spirit permission to receive the set of instructions for our "next." However, if we are afraid of our fears and do not admit before God what is bothering us, we will continue to lie to ourselves and even believe our own inaccuracies. Unfortunately, many people spend their lives in the cave of their own fears because they are unwilling to acknowledge their mistakes or admit they may have inaccurate views about God. They are unwilling to ask for His help to open their eyes to His truth.

Notice that God always finds you, even while you hide in embarrassment and fear. He draws you close to Himself by securing the harness, even pulling the parachute handle if you forget. His desire is to reveal His love to you on a greater level, to coax you out of your cave of pain and welcome you into the shelter of His presence. Listen for Him to give you His instructions for your upcoming destination.

Elijah needed a new direction. The Lord gave him the next order and with that, new hope was released in his spirit. The clouds of oppression began to dissipate, and he could see and hear once again.

ESCAPING THE TRAP OF SELF-SABOTAGE

When traveling internationally through crowded cities, I am always aware of the dangers of pickpocketing. Most of the time we advise team members traveling with us to leave their valuables in a safe location to prevent theft of their identity or finances. You can be blindsided in the most surprising ways, not realizing that someone standing next to you is robbing you. As vigilant as we are to protect our personal belongings from theft, how much more important is it for us to guard our inner peace and vision?

Sometimes, in the spiritual sense, it's not someone reaching in to steal, it's us handing it to them without discretion. Emotionally immature visionaries often end up sharing too much information. Perhaps,

at the wrong time,

with the wrong people.

Or possibly,

at the right time,

with the wrong people.

We live in a restless society that demands instant information and immediate results.

As a result, we are under constant pressure to communicate our new ideas quickly and impress others. Instead of protecting an idea or dream, we sometimes share it too soon. Like skydiving from a plane, we are flying with our mouths wide open and are quickly running out of oxygen. Our sustainability is decreased, but we don't even realize it until our creativity is dry and our insecurities disclosed. It doesn't look pleasant, but because we can't see our own blind spots, we treat them as our assets while those around us pretend not to notice.

When our hearts are attuned to the Holy Spirit—the Guide who whispers in our ear as we glide in the safety of the harness—He will prompt us to share our ideas and dreams when the time is right, and let us know with whom to share them: those who will support, celebrate, and even help launch the dream. When we don't wait for His cue, we are robbing ourselves of the
> happiness,
> > harmony,
> > > and fulfillment
> > > > our dreams are meant to bring us.

In 2012, I had the honor of briefly meeting the Jesuit theologian and philosopher Father Robert Spitzer. Based on his research on human behavior, he categorizes happiness on four levels, from lower to higher. While each level is good, the higher the level a person attains, the greater the depth of happiness expressed in life.

Level 1 is defined as the happiness achieved through short-term, instant gratification: enjoying a great meal, watching your favorite TV show, purchasing something you've always wanted. It is short-lived, without any deep meaningful application.

Level 2 stems from personal achievement and ego gratification. Usually we strive for this level by believing that "I would be happy if..." So we pursue a degree, a well-paid career, an award for accomplishment, personal goals, marriage, children, or other symbols of happiness. Unfortunately, the next big thing in life will never satisfy us. Father Spitzer states that when this level "becomes your only goal, it leads to self-absorption, jealousy, fear of failure, contempt, isolation, and cynicism."[3]

In Level 3, happiness is derived from doing good for others out of empathy rather than selfishness. While this level unites us in our pursuit of moral ideals, it has its limits, since we are imperfect beings who cannot find fulfillment in the imperfections of others.

---

[3] "The Four Levels Defined," Spitzer Center, SpitzerCenter.org.

It's easy to run out of breath when you become addicted to the pursuit of happiness found only in Levels 1 and 2. In addition, if your desire is to land as soon as possible just to bask in the applause of human recognition, then your Level 3 happiness will quickly come to an end. Even at Level 3, it is easy for us to think—like Elijah—that we are the only ones left or chosen by God to fulfill His plan. We may start off with high ideals but disconnect ourselves in the process and live at a lower level because we didn't understand the seasons of change and development of our character.

Perfect happiness is found in Level 4, a longing for "ultimacy," or a connection with something or someone greater than ourselves. This level represents "the perfect, unrestricted and eternal happiness that comes from union with God."[4] His "grace of divine love" eventually helps us to properly enjoy the lower levels of happiness while on this earth.[5]

Bulgarians will always remember and honor the courage of Vasil Levski, a revolutionary Orthodox monk who sacrificed his personal ambition for the freedom of his nation. During the 500-year rule of the Ottoman Empire, Levski rose to the call to free the Bulgarian people from oppression. He envisioned Bulgaria as a democratic republic where people from all religious groups and ethnicities would live with equal rights and liberties—a radical and dangerous concept to the ruling class.

It was rare for anyone living under bondage at that time to think on the level of liberation. Levski's faith in Christ gave him the fearless approach to live beyond happiness Levels 1, 2, and 3 and to do everything in life out of connection with God's greater purpose. He inspired more than 1,000 others from all strata of society to join in the same mission.[6] For their own safety, each person had to understand their importance and commitment within the organization and protect one another.[7] Unfortunately, betrayal is common in high-risk environments and even the most strong-willed can give up under torture, beatings, and emotional distress. Levski was betrayed, caught, and sentenced to death by hanging at age 35.

But his death was not in vain. Inspired by his courage, many more arose to fight, joining together even while their bodies were weary and their faith dim. Through his death, Levski passed his mantle on to a generation prepared to hear, believe, and act. Five years later, on March 3, 1878, Bulgaria was liberated from the Ottoman Empire during the Russian-Turkish war.

---

[4] *Presentation on Creation* home page, Spitzer Center, SpitzerCenter.org.
[5] Ibid.
[6] "Commemoration of Vassil Levski," TheInfoList.com.
[7] Neuburger, *The American Historical Review*, 89–90.

A similar principle of legacy is reflected in the life of Elijah. Doubting his future, his own calling, and even God's presence in his life, he went down the path of desiring death. A redeemed thought process emerged only when he was able to die to his false belief that he alone was left to preserve Israel. God had not forgotten Elijah. Before he even realized his need for partnership, the Lord had prepared Elisha to join Elijah on the journey by becoming his disciple and later his successor.

In skydiving, I noticed that experienced skydivers jump together. While they are still at high elevation, they form beautiful figures in the sky by holding hands with one another. When it is time to release their parachutes, they let go so they don't become entangled or collide. This is the level of operation and partnership to which God is calling us:

> To sustain one another,
>> not compete.
>>> To elevate the gifts of others,
>>>> not suppress.
>>>>> To release them into
>>>>>> greatness and potential,
>>>>>>> not withhold blessings.

LETTING GO OF THE CONTROLLED PLAN

"If I win, I win for the entire people. If I lose, I lose only myself."

For nineteen years, I passed by the monument of Vasil Levski located near my home. Almost daily I read these powerful words engraved in stone, sometimes in the rush of catching a bus, other times resting in the grass at the park. They became an invisible mentor in my life. But due to my limited understanding, these same words drove me to a place of despair. You could say I found myself in a similar situation to that of Elijah.

Inspired by Levski and other Bulgarian and international heroes who fought for the liberation of nations, I had set high goals and aspirations. Everything

Vasil Levski monument – Veliko Turnovo, Bulgaria

within me was working toward the realization of these goals. Each time I would achieve one, however, I would go through days or weeks of emotional letdown. Unable to explain what was happening to me, I kept constantly busy with traveling and meetings. Over the years, I've come to the conclusion that busyness is a masked desperation to hide our dissatisfaction. That was true in my life, and with it I spiraled into a dark depression.

Shortly after my 35th birthday, I woke up one day in a tangle of negative, depressing thoughts accompanied by deep exhaustion. They quickly intensified in a suicidal frenzy that I had been suppressing in my mind. Somehow, I had subconsciously connected my own life with Levski's and decided that I, too, would die at age 35. To make matters worse, I returned home from a speaking tour to find my condo flooded. A snowstorm had frozen all the pipes in the building. The belongings I had left were placed in storage, and I moved into a hotel for the next four months.

After two months of gray skies and nonstop rain in Seattle, my hotel stay began to wear on me. It was Christmastime, and I had the same feelings of abandonment as when I had first arrived in the States. They triggered negative responses in my mind and body. I was like Elijah, hidden in the cave of my hotel room, when the Lord asked me, "What are you doing here?"

My simple answer followed: "I am the only one who feels like this. No one understands me. Everyone else is having a wonderful time celebrating Christmas with their families and I am at a hotel. Alone! I have done everything I needed to do on this earth, and I don't feel like living anymore." My pity party continued for a few more hours, but thankfully, I did not act on those feelings. Just like God came and rescued Elijah out of his cave, He rescued me from my loneliness, fears, and suicidal thoughts.

The next twenty-four hours were crucial. By the next afternoon, my life had been transformed from devastation to hope through one phone call. That was the day I was introduced to The Pacific Institute and met Lou and Diane Tice. I was brought to them through unusual circumstances during the darkest hours of my journey. The "letting go" of my controlled plan was the new start in the release of God's higher revelation and repositioning for the next phase of my life.

Before you continue reading, take a moment to ask yourself, *Have I disconnected the harness keeping me tied to God's purpose? Am I in a state of self-sabotage? Am I willing to make a conscious effort to change my thought patterns?* The good news is that positive adjustments can be made at any time. But you are the only one who can decide to make them.

If you have experienced dark seasons in your life and felt hopelessness, it is my sincere prayer and desire that you consciously choose to embrace some of these truths and suggested strategies. If you have been struggling with severe depression, I encourage you to seek the help of a doctor or professional therapist.

TRUTHS

1. **God is for you.** He is a faithful, loving Savior who has your best solution in mind and loves you eternally. "'Though the mountains be shaken and the hills be removed, yet my unfailing love for you will not be shaken nor my covenant of peace be removed,' says the LORD, who has compassion on you" (Isaiah 54:10 NIV).

2. **You are not alone.** Even if you are questioning, Where is God when I need Him? the truth is, God is always with you. "Where can I go from your Spirit? .... If I say, 'Surely the darkness will hide me and the light become night around me,' even the darkness will not be dark to you; the night will shine like the day, for darkness is as light to you" (Psalm 139:7, 11–12 NIV).

3. **You are not the only one to feel this way**—many of the people we revere in the Bible have lost heart and walked this same path of discouragement. Yet their lives can serve as an example and encouragement to us as we see that even in the most desperate circumstances, God can—and will—restore hope.

4. **Know your enemy.** The devil may try to speak lies and destruction into your life, but Jesus brings abundant life. "'The thief comes only to steal and kill and destroy; I have come that they may have life, and have it to the full'"(John 10:10 NIV).

5. **When all seems dark, remember the One** whose Word is a lamp to our feet and a light to our path (Psalm 119:105). In the words of King David, "You, LORD, are my lamp; the LORD turns my darkness into light" (2 Samuel 22:29 NIV). He delights in rescuing us and bringing us from despair to new life.

SUGGESTED STRATEGIES

1. **Search out God's promises in Scripture.** The Bible is full of comfort, hope, and the blessing of His love. "He heals the brokenhearted and binds up their wounds" (Psalm 147:3).[8]

2. **Learn to let negative feelings pass without acting on them.** Feelings are temporary. (In fact, they come and go in 90-second intervals.[9]) Sometimes only an hour or even a few minutes can make a significant difference in your perception of your situation.

3. **Don't make a permanent decision to solve a temporary problem.** Whatever you are facing is only a shadow of the truth; at this time you are only seeing fragments of the whole picture.

4. **Avoid self-talk in negative absolutes** such as "the only one," "no one else," "left alone," or "never." These phrases are a sign that you have entered a destructive emotional spiral. Instead, choose to speak or write positive messages: "I am not alone; God is with me!" "I am not the only one! I can and I will make it!" "I will never give up!"

5. **Remember a moment in your life when you felt fulfilled, happy, and excited,** and allow those feelings to stir up additional fulfilling memories. This will give you a recovery point, which triggers courage instead of negativity. Take a few minutes to write down what you appreciate and value in your life. On days when you feel hopeless, read what you have written as a reminder.

6. **You are still loved and needed on this earth!** Give yourself a small, immediate goal. Get dressed and get out of bed; take a walk in a park or in an area with people, even if you don't feel like it. Choose to disrupt your negative train of thought by reading the Bible or an uplifting book, watching an inspiring and lighthearted movie, or turning on music that is positive and soothing.

---

[8] Additional Scriptures that bring hope: Deut. 33:27; Psalm 23:4; 27:14; 32: 7–9; Psalm 34; Isaiah 26: 3–4.

[9] Siegel and Bryson, *The Whole-Brain Child*, 103.

THE TRANSITION FROM "ME" TO "WE"

As I mentioned, the gliding time with my instructor was of great importance for the safety in our descent. I needed to have a clear picture in my mind of the transition process, and I needed to trust my guide. The longer I hesitated to promise that I would allow him to land on his feet first, the longer we kept gliding.

Similar to skydiving, something supernatural transpires inside of us during the process of waiting on God and trusting Him. Isaiah 40:31 gives us a glimpse of the strength and renewal we receive for the journey ahead: "Those who wait on the LORD shall renew their strength; they shall mount up with wings like eagles, they shall run and not be weary, they shall walk and not faint."

The actual word "wait" in Hebrew is *qavah*, and it means to bind together by twisting; to expect, gather together, look patiently for, wait for or upon.[10] The binding by twisting is like two ropes being twisted together so that they are no longer distinguished as two, but appear as one—interconnected and inseparable, increased in strength and longevity.[11]

An interesting process happens in our minds when we watch the actions of another. In neuroscience, the term "mirror neuron" is used to describe the response of neurons that permit us to mimic the behavior of another person as well as vibrate their emotional state.[12]

These neurons respond only to a perceived purpose of intention. According to the authors of *The Whole-Brain Child*, "We don't just 'mirror back' to someone else, but we 'sponge in' their internal states."[13] Because we are relational beings, our minds are created to adopt important aspects of the thinking, acting, responding, and behavioral processes of those around us. Furthermore, through that process, we "join our individual 'me' with others to become a part of 'we.'"[14]

Since our brain responds on this level of assimilation with the behavior of others, likewise, the longer we "glide" and spend time with the Lord, the more our neurons begin to mirror the supernatural character and likeness of God. If God did not exist and we were to believe in the idea of a god (as defined by any religion), then the

---

[10] Strong's Hebrew: 6960 (qavah).
[11] For additional information on Isaiah 40:31, see Steven P. Wickstrom, "Wait upon the Lord," Spwickstrom, http://www.spwickstrom.com/wait/.
[12] Siegel and Bryson, *The Whole-Brain Child*, 124.
[13] Ibid., 125.
[14] Ibid.

mirror neuron would only adopt information based on that particular religion without any emotional mirroring. However, for both behavioral and emotional change to transpire, the mirror neuron must be connected with the actual presence and existence of a person. Because Christ lives within us, we can reflect his character, confidence, compassion, power, and the rest of His attributes.

As you become entwined with God, you will mirror hope from Him,[15] rather than despair from within yourself or from the world around you. Only then, upon "landing," can you speak and live

> out of the release of His strength for the weary,
> out of His compassion for the brokenhearted,
> out of the passion of His vision for humanity,
> out of being as one with Him!

---

[15] Colossians 1:26–27.

AN EXPERIENTIAL IMAGERY EXERCISE

You may color it and write in the open space of the graphic, or inside the cartoon's mouth, the dreams or goals that have been lost or stolen due to various circumstances.

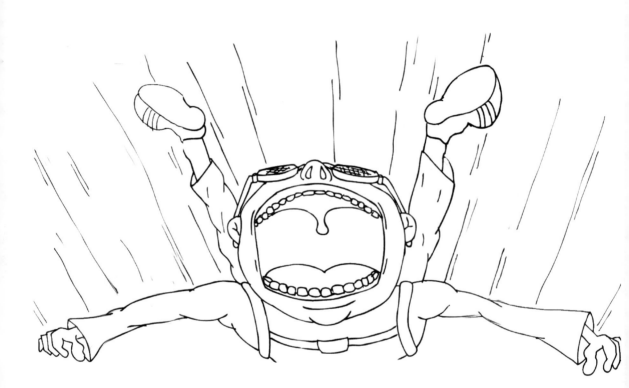

PRINCIPLE

Listen to the Holy Spirit's direction of when, how, and with whom to share your dreams and goals. Learn to embrace the season of "gliding" to rest in the Lord and let Him prepare you for your next assignment. Forethought and proper planning, even of the seasons of rest, will sustain the emotional, mental, and spiritual momentum in your life.

Take the time to think about the areas of your life in which you have lost momentum because you failed to exercise forethought and set new goals. *In the left column, write the areas in which you wish to reset your goals. On the right side, across from each area, write a practical action step. It may be just a few words or a sentence that would help you trigger excitement and regain your drive. If you wish to write about areas where you need downtime, you may include what you see yourself doing during that season. Stay positive, optimistic, and prayerful in the process.*

I would like to reset my goals in these areas:	Practical action steps:
Example: Exercise	**Example:** Finding someone to exercise with 3 times a week OR finding a trainer for $___per/month

I am choosing to rest in the following areas:	**My downtime would look like (use a few words to describe):**

LIBERATED FROM INVISIBLE CRUTCHES

AND NO LONGER IN SEARCH OF YOUR TRAINING WHEELS

chapter

> "The **reason** I didn't give up on God when I put away my other imaginary friends is that every time I create more room by vacating an imaginary friend, I find more space for those extraordinary encounters with the living God."[1]

– ERWIN MCMANUS

THE SOUND of the gypsy's fiddle mixed with whistles, clapping, and laughter woke me from my afternoon nap. Sprinting to the nearest window of the bedroom, my heart raced as I realized I was missing the action outside.

During my childhood, gypsies commonly traveled from house to house, predominantly in the village areas outside the busy city life. They would ask for various items—clothes, food, or money—while entertaining their audience through a variety of talents. I recognized the elderly gypsy in ragged clothes standing in my grandparents' backyard; he had stopped by our house in the past. With undeveloped skills but a heart filled with passion, he always performed as though my family and neighbors were the only audience in the entire world worthy of his attention. His face portrayed the deep sorrow of his heart while his eyes welled up with tears each time he stretched forth his hand to beg.

---

[1] McManus, *The Artisan Soul,* 100.

This time the man had brought his dancing bear—one of his added methods of survival. To secure the animal, a thick rope connected the gypsy's left wrist to a heavy, rusty chain wrapped around the right leg of the skinny brown bear. In a way, the chain mirrored the degradation and cruelty suffered under such poverty for both the gypsy and the animal.

Dashing out of my bedroom, I rushed to catch the opportunity to dance next to the bear. Unfortunately, the gypsy had already completed his repertoire and was headed to the neighbors' home. I jumped on my bike and pedaled furiously over the hill to reach their house before his arrival. I wanted to be part of the new audience to greet him and the bear as they approached. And there he was, nearing slowly, as the sounds of the fiddle announced his arrival. Kids from the neighborhood gathered in a circle and we danced and leaped to the beat of the music.

Embracing those moments in life and finding joy in their simplicity relieved the bleakness of our existence. We lived without luxury but never lacked imagination. We knew how to create a dance without music,
> and a song without words.
> > How to find the beauty of life
> > > while stomping in the dirt.
How to play with the animals,
> the insects, and our imaginary friends
> > who would never betray the secrets of our hearts.

My father's voice interrupted my euphoria. "Dinner is ready—get back home!" he called. The echo transformed his words into a shout that carried over the streets.

I hopped on my bike, stirring up the settled dust as I flew toward home. My parents and grandparents were waiting outside the house for my arrival. I looked back to see if anyone else was following. *Oh, no! What? My dad removed the training wheels from my bike?!*

The very moment I realized those little wheels were missing, I fell to the ground. Rolling into the dust, I scratched my knees and elbows. *Why*

Happy moments cruising on my bike.

didn't he ask my permission? How could he do this to me? I angrily punched the ground with my fist.

With a smile, my dad came running toward me. He dusted me off, lifted me up, and carried me in one arm while dragging the bike with his other hand. "You did just fine without the training wheels," he said, "until you looked back and realized they were missing—that's when you lost your balance and fell. I removed them because I've been watching you ride for a long time and you have outgrown them. They are preventing you from going faster around the curves and are holding you back. You don't need them."

> Just a few words,
> > spoken during a brief conversation,
> > > left an impact
> > > > that has remained with me
> > > > > through the years.

We all want to live a life of freedom—to ride our bikes as fast as we can in order to achieve all that we could imagine. We start off with training wheels attached. Sometimes we can't wait to be adults and ride without them. But other times, we mistakenly embrace what was meant to be temporary as a permanent support. The same freedom we so deeply desired when we were children we now fearfully push aside. Instead of letting go of what we've outgrown, we add on more! More tools or relationships or possessions to carry and sustain us along the pathway of life. We tolerate what hinders us, and even ignore it, because we are afraid to look into the darker areas of our souls.

What brought joy to us now ushers in annoyance, and what we used to value we now disregard because of lack of time. We disconnect from truly loving, feeling, and listening because the fast pace of life demands our attention. And one day we wake up, only to find ourselves changed from carefree children with a song in our hearts to adults who hear the pronounced static noise our life has become. After all,

> how could we risk in love
> > and dare to be vulnerable?
> > > How could we risk for others
> > > > and dare to forgive?

No matter how hard we try to protect our loved ones and ourselves from life's dangers, we can't avoid pain, sorrow, loss, or emptiness. Somewhere along the way we failed to understand the voices of our invisible mentors, and we used them instead as crutches—justifying the excuses that stifled our emotional and spiritual growth.

One of our natural inclinations is to run, to escape that which confines us—what we consciously or unconsciously have adopted to rely upon. We may secretly resent our life of self-imposed confinement but not know how to throw aside the crutches—outwardly hidden, yet inwardly supporting what we fear to let go of. Because to let go would require us to embrace a different life. A life of

a higher level of thinking,
a greater level of serving, and
a deeper level of love—
toward God,
toward ourselves,
toward others.
Dismissing the training wheels,
leaving the imaginary friends,
discarding the invisible crutches.

MEETING JESUS AT THE WELL OF OUR SOUL

Like any good parent, God knows our gifts and our potential. He gives us our talents, abilities, and creativity and calls us to a life beyond the dirt road of our childhood. He stirs our curiosity and leaves it to our imagination to add the "and also" to all we can be.

With the purest of love for us, God sees our brokenness and knows which training wheels of our lives must be removed for us to experience greater joy and freedom. When liberated on the inside, we will eventually exchange our invisible crutches for the revelation that

He is endless.
He is timeless.
He is limitless.
Therefore, the truth we discover through new
opportunities and challenges
will continuously expand our knowledge.
It will stretch the confines of
our past realities.
More so, it will reveal the truth in the person of Jesus,[2]
and our eyes will be open to see Him.

On a hot, sunny day, tired from His journey, Jesus stopped at Jacob's well outside the

---

[2] "Jesus said to [Thomas], 'I am the way, the truth, and the life. No one comes to the Father except through Me'" (John 14:6).

town of Sychar. No one was expected to be there. As soon as He stopped, she appeared. Alone.

Bringing her burdens
inside her empty jars.

The longest one-on-one conversation of Jesus recorded in the New Testament is with a woman whose name remains unknown.[3] Perceived as unclean by the Jews because she was a Samaritan, she arrived at the well during a time she suspected no one would be there to judge her. Trying to escape any potential social gatherings where questions would be asked or gossip spread about her, she lived in the isolation of her dark soul cave. From the outside, no one could imagine the miracle that was set in motion. Not even her. For she was barely enduring life in an ocean of rejection created by her social environment and perhaps by her personal choices.

But Jesus was about to transform her life from a place of survival to a place of certainty, of validation, and of dignity. The story she had been telling herself for years—

a story of failure,
a story of loss,
a story of defeat—

was about to be changed into a powerful testament proclaiming the freedom of every woman and every man.

> Jesus said to her, "Give Me a drink." For His disciples had gone away into the city to buy food. Then the woman of Samaria said to Him, "How is it that You, being a Jew, ask a drink from me, a Samaritan woman?" For Jews have no dealings with Samaritans. Jesus answered and said to her, "If you knew the gift of God, and who it is who says to you, 'Give Me a drink,' you would have asked Him, and He would have given you living water."

> The woman said to Him, "Sir, You have nothing to draw with, and the well is deep. Where then do You get that living water? Are You greater than our father Jacob, who gave us the well, and drank from it himself, as well as his sons and his livestock?" Jesus answered and said to her, "Whoever drinks of this water will thirst again, but whoever drinks of the water that I shall give him will never thirst. But the water that I shall give him will become in him a fountain of water springing up into everlasting life." The woman said to Him, "Sir, give me this water, that I may not thirst, nor come here to draw" (John 4:7b-14).

I view this passage as the ultimate expression of the true, loving qualities of a relational

---

[3] John 4:5–42.

God. It is important for us to understand that first of all, He is always available to speak with us individually. Secondly, He will remain in the conversation until He has transitioned us from a place of anxiety to a refuge of safety. He is never uncomfortable with our imperfections. Thirdly, nothing we have done or will do intimidates Him or causes Him to reject us. He is intimately involved in the details of our lives. We are often afraid of closeness because we are afraid of being hurt. But Jesus neutralizes that fear. He knows we need recovery from each instance of hurt in our lives—each person or event that has harmed us. Those memories must heal so they don't remain painful wounds, bleeding in our lives.

Fourth, He bypasses any religious, cultural, and human mind-sets that cause us to live in isolation from one another. He seals the cracks of our fragmented souls, exchanging our broken picture of reality with His solid, whole one. He shows us perfection based on His reality, character, and unrestricted love.

Later in this story, Jesus takes the woman's focus away from the law and traditional rituals that had brought so much condemnation and pain to her life. He inquires about her husband but knew that she was living with a sixth man without being married to him—her social crutch for survival. Before any misconceptions are made about her, it's necessary to understand that she was living within the bounds of cultural disadvantages. Women were not respected at that time. The only way for her to survive was to be married. We don't know the reasons the previous five men were no longer in her life; it could have been death or divorce, or simply rejection. Women were so reliant on men for their survival that they were not usually the initiators of a breakup.

Jesus did not bring up her marital status to make her appear a sinner. Quite the contrary. He brought it out in the open so He could reposition her identity beyond the cultural crutch of her existence. He spoke to her first from the position of a man who was also a Jew, and secondly, by asking her to offer Him a drink from Jacob's well. Both of these broke the cultural restrictions of who she was, yet the only way to truly validate her identity was for Him to reveal His own. Jesus is always the first one to take a step of transparency in order for us to lose our insecurity in His acceptance. The instant her eyes were opened to see the emptiness of her soul's "well"—the broken pieces of her life—the numbing static noise of her circumstances transformed into a melody of liberation and hope.

The crutches of culture, religion, or the labels others have put on us are not greater than Jesus. If we think they are, then we solidify our pain and discard the hope of change. We dismiss the power of God's love and, intentionally or not, embrace the power of an addiction instead. Addictions give us a false sense of release from pain and an illusion of comfort. They take place in our life

> when the emptiness of our souls,
>> the loneliness of our hearts,
>>> the tears in our eyes,
> are left unmet,
>> unspoken,
>>> unseen.

Addictions are like putting helium inside our soul—
> we fly high, but we are hollow;
>> we are seen, but we are not sustained.

We feel attached,
> but only by a string connecting us
>> to the broken pieces of our souls.

When we bury our pain while our heart is still crying, we lose our voice to speak. It's like getting laryngitis; the swelling in our throats prevents the release of the sound. We know we've arrived at the dry well of our life when

> we reach for help, but no one sees us;
>> we speak, but no one hears us.

We hide behind the invisible crutches and training wheels of our bikes, tired of taking another curve in life without enough power to face tomorrow. We hold on to empty attachments and to past pleasant experiences, hoping that our imagination is strong enough to sustain their invisible empowerment.

The unnamed Samaritan woman will be remembered as the first evangelist to go into the city and proclaim that Jesus was the Messiah.

> All she had was a story.
>> All she needed was a voice.
>> All she did was use it.

Her experiences were redeemed as the "Word became flesh"[4] and made a permanent dwelling, filling up her empty jars with living water.

When your cries for validation are heard in the secret meeting at the well that you have with God, you can stop seeking external approval. Christ empowers us to own our story and to own our pain. Because of Him, we have permission to embrace our scars and become the greatest testifiers to our own lives. Just like the Samaritan woman. At that point, our trauma from painful experiences no longer carries the contamination of self-judgment and self-condemnation. Like her, we are led to cleanse ourselves in

---

[4] John 1:14.

God's ocean of grace and mercy. It gives us the power to reflect on our scars and find the accurate meaning for our stories.

It is in that moment that the miracle transpires: our invisible crutches are redeemed to become our invisible mentors. We are no longer lost in our painful memories, with distorted thinking and lost identities. The history of our life, good or bad, cannot be altered, but our future can be changed as we allow God's living waters to flow into the deserted places of our hearts. His love resurrects a new message within us.

> A message that is powerful.
> A message that brings deliverance.
> A message that establishes a new freedom
> not only within us,
> but also in others.

Jesus wakes us up in time to hear the sound of new music. We won't miss the dance. He tells us that the life we have lived half-alert is no longer good enough. That just around the corner of the dirt road is a change in scenery. And as soon as we lift up our heads and feel His embrace, the sound of joyous worship will flow from us. Worship not based on religion or someone else's experience but grounded "in spirit and truth."[5] Worship that will challenge us to leave our small-minded human perceptions of ourselves and others at the well, because we have seen Him—our personal Messiah—and can now walk in greater freedom and purpose.

SILENCING THE VOICE OF FEAR

Sun rays slipped through the blinds of my bedroom, welcoming a new day. I woke from a restless sleep, the familiar burden of grief leaving my heart lonely and sad.

The death of my mom only four months after her cancer diagnosis had been quick and devastating. She passed away on Easter morning, a few hours before one of my speaking engagements. On Good Friday and all day Saturday, I had been dealing with the perplexity in my heart. I had to release her. I had promised her over the phone that I'd take care of my dad. At that time, she could no longer speak but she was willing to fight through this battle. I struggled to make sense of all that was happening, replaying the situation in slow motion, searching for answers. While we know that death is inevitable, somehow we never really think it will happen to us or to our loved ones.

Since I was in a different country at the time, I couldn't be present for her funeral.[6]

---

[5] "'God is Spirit, and those who worship Him must worship in spirit and truth'" (John 4:24).
[6] Funerals in Bulgaria take place 24–48 hours after the person dies because the bodies are not embalmed or cremated.

Though I wrote a speech and saw pictures from her memorial service, in my mind the reality was not one of death. I had absolute peace in my heart that she was with the Lord, and to a great extent, that eased the pain. However, with time, the strength of my imagination and memories of my mom did not permit me to grieve her earthly departure in a healthy way.

Shortly after her passing, I moved from the Midwest to the West Coast. Yet no matter how many miles I traveled, the pain traveled with me. And however many plane rides I took to disconnect myself from the earthly burdens, the heaviness of my sorrow always found its way onto each flight. Not only did the shadows of pain follow me, but they established permanent residence in my mind. Instead of rejecting them, I gave them a voice. While I had lost many things in my life, I had never dealt with the pain of losing a person so dear to my heart. I wasn't sure how to process the experience and grieve through it.

No matter how big or small,
No matter whether inflicted by a person,
by conflicts, or by circumstances,
any loss can create
trauma and lingering emotional anguish.

Afraid of the pain, I created an invisible, permanent reality of my mom in my mind. It would have been understandable if she was the only one living there, but my thoughts were also occupied with others who, over time, had left my life due to various circumstances. The fear of feeling lonely and alone created a void that I filled with my imagination.

Each day, I would recall certain memories
when I needed comfort,
when I felt like I was lost,
or when I thought I was alone.

I could go for days living in my head, oblivious to what was happening in the world. Externally, I was accomplishing a lot, but emotionally I was frozen in time. My traveling schedule became impossible to manage as I bounced from one place to the next, trying to escape reality.

A close friend spoke truth to me: "You have to make room for your future to come in. Your calendar is so full, you have no time for rest. Anything new gets suffocated amid all the appointments." In a way, my calendar was an addiction that was feeding the invisible crutches. After all, I was outwardly "saving the world," but inwardly I was suppressing my fears.

In our most vulnerable times such as loss of a loved one, a broken relationship, or financial difficulties, fear may try to take over your thoughts. No matter how strong you are and how well equipped to control your thoughts, fear can sneak in. It will wake you from sleep in a cold sweat or cloud your perspective. You lose your sense of peace. It causes you to spin inside the circle of pain, without a pathway to safety. Fear suffocates your dreams.

But fear cannot silence the voice of Jesus. He knows exactly when to show up and how to speak to our fears. He gives us direction. If we want to find the way out of our own darkness, we must ask for His help and guidance.

As I lay in bed that sunlit morning, God met me at the empty well of my soul.

> *You are simply afraid of being alone. Therefore, you have created invisible crutches that are occupying your thoughts and in reality holding you back. Unless you let them go, you will not be able to embrace anything new I am bringing into your life. Not because you don't have time, but because you don't have space. Your mind is occupied by the false reality of the existence of people and old opportunities that are not even connected to you anymore.*

Only God would have known something so private about me to challenge my belief. Yet He cared enough to expose it in order to help me walk out of the valley of grief. His love filled my heart with serenity and sweet peace. I still had questions, but somehow I also had all the answers I needed. I knew that at last I could release the deep pain of my grief and find healing. He was my only safe refuge.

REDEMPTION OF A CULTURE

According to Dr. Bessel van der Kolk, one of the world's leading experts in the field of PTSD (post-traumatic stress disorder), only 5 percent[7] of those who survived the 9/11 attack in New York experienced PTSD. Comparison was made with survivors of Hurricane Katrina in New Orleans, where 33 percent suffered these symptoms.[8] Both events, though different circumstantially, were devastating and had a traumatic impact on individuals, families, and the entire society.

Why are the percentages so different if both experiences contained trauma and loss? The conclusion is that the survivors of 9/11 had the opportunity to openly grieve by returning to see the ruins after the attack. In addition, they received national support

---

[7] Van der Kolk, "Keynote Session: Complex Trauma," YouTube Video.
[8] Patel, "Hurricane Katrina survivors," Princeton University.

through media coverage. Everyone who died or survived the aftermath of the attack was pronounced a national hero. On the other hand, the powerful hurricane took the lives and homes of many who were mostly minority civilians from low-income families. Because of damage and contamination from the flooding, the survivors could not return to their area of residency. Most of them were displaced to other cities and states. The media portrayed them as victims and unfortunately, that label lowered their coping skills and their resilience in recovering from the trauma.[9]

According to *Psychology Today*: "We rely not just on our loved ones and our immediate family, but our entire community and culture when recovering from a major traumatic social event. The likelihood of a survivor experiencing PTSD as a result of a trigger event depends not just on the event itself, but on the ensuing circumstances and the cultural reaction to the event."[10]

When an entire community and culture grieve together it creates a place of safety for everyone and healing takes place faster. Further, our pain from traumatic experiences releases a sense of empowerment within us, signaling to our mind and emotions that we are not alone, when it is
> remembered,
>> acknowledged, and
>>> met with empathy.

Considering again the woman at the well, could we say that the miracle Jesus did in her heart was solidified when she returned and shared it with her community? Was it the experience of her liberation that shifted the Samaritan culture into a position of empowerment? Her return into the city disturbed their frozen-in-time trauma, infused by the cultural rejection of the Jews. The only way for freedom to be released was for their pain to be remembered, acknowledged openly, and empathized with by someone similar to them, who
> experienced loss,
>> experienced rejection, and
>>> experienced acceptance.

The woman met Jesus as a victim but returned as a hero. Her words, "Come, see a Man who told me all things that I ever did. Could this be the Christ?" (John 4:29) were spoken with boldness from a personal revelation, while her fears were drowned in the well of God's empathy. She went alone into the city but came back with an entire community.

---

[9] Babbel, "Post Traumatic Stress Disorder After 9/11 and Katrina," *Psychology Today.*
[10] Ibid. Additional studies on the effects of 9/11 can be found at https://www.ncbi.nlm.nih.gov/pmc/articles/PMC3386850/.

They desired to hear these same words, "He told me all that I ever did…"
They looked for the same acceptance at the well of living water.

Their dignity was restored and their pain was healed as they cried and rejoiced together upon meeting Jesus. "Then they said to the woman, 'Now we believe, not because of what you said, for we ourselves have heard Him and we know that this is indeed the Christ, the Savior of the world'" (John 4:42). Jesus shifted an entire culture from a *victim* mind-set to a *victor* mind-set—heroes who discovered the Savior of the world.

When He spoke to them,
they felt understood.
When He embraced them,
they felt accepted.
When He released them,
they felt empowered.

FREEDOM FROM THE INVISIBLE CRUTCHES

Unless we realize that "the only things we can keep are the things we freely give to God,"[11] we will continue to live within the confines of our secrets. The fear of letting go of our invisible crutches is often greater than the reality of life without them. While meditating on what God said to me, a new thought emerged. Everything in my life that I was holding on to—people, possessions, my ministry, my schedule—needed to be visually and physically disconnected from me. Like the Samaritan woman, I had to find the well and leave my empty jars there.

And so I did.

I headed to the nearest beach in downtown Seattle to gather some stones. As I approached the pier that faced the Cascade mountains, I looked up and whispered, "This is it. I am finally going to let go of my invisible crutches." I took each stone and gave it a name—a person, situation, even a regret—and I threw them into the water one by one. As each stone was swallowed into the ocean depths, the waters received my burdens and I felt as if thousands of pounds had fallen off my shoulders. I was free from the emotional ache and the invisible crutches that cluttered my mind. The painful facts of the experiences transitioned safely into healed memories in the storehouse of my subconscious.

The day I found the courage to let go of my invisible crutches was the day my grief became a mentor in my life. To grieve is not a lack of faith and dependence on God.

---

[11] Lewis, *Complete C.S. Lewis Signature Classics,* 168.

Healthy grief must be experienced through identifying the loss and allowing yourself to feel it fully. The sadness of losing someone you love never goes away completely, but as time passes, these emotions become less intense as you accept the loss and start to move forward.

Somehow, what I let go of with my own hands opened the door of my heart to be flooded with God's love. Through that encounter, I came to understand at a much more intimate level the words of the Samaritan woman, "He told me all that I ever did," and He patiently waited for me to let go of the invisible in order to recognize the One: my Messiah—the Savior of my soul.

Ask yourself this important question: Is what you are holding on to so tightly only temporarily sustaining you—like a crutch—without the power to eternally uphold you? If the answer is yes, then it's time to choose to release it to God. His love will transform the static noise in your life into a beautiful melody, and He will teach you the dance steps to the new beat.

Take a deep breath.

Close your eyes.

Feel the breeze.

You've been liberated from the invisible crutches.

No longer in search of the training wheels,

you can ride forth without any hindrance.

AN EXPERIENTIAL IMAGERY EXERCISE

Identify the names of your invisible crutches—people, possessions, memories, even pain in your life that you need to release to God. Using one or two words, write each one inside the stones in this graphic.

Besides writing it on paper, you may want to take action in a symbolic way, as I did with stones at the beach. Be creative! God can meet you anytime, anywhere. He just wants you to come and allow Him to silence your fears.

PRINCIPLE

When we don't take the opportunity to identify our fears, we create and hold on to our invisible crutches. Through Christ we are transitioned from a place of emotional emptiness or traumatic loss to a place of recovery and complete liberation. We can cast our invisible crutches into the well of Living Water as Jesus reveals His identity to us and we experience safety and acceptance.

Take time to think through the process:

What are your fears?

Which invisible crutches are holding you back? What are you holding on to that is preventing you from growing in certain areas of your life?

Specifically identify the people and circumstances that have been invisible crutches in your life. What are some practical steps you would like to take in order to release them to God and experience healing?

How has Jesus revealed Himself to you? It may be through a Scripture you have read, a song you heard, a quiet voice speaking to your heart, or a specific awareness of His presence. Take time to pray and reflect on those moments—they will edify and encourage you.

7

FINDING RESTORATION

WHEN ALL SEEMS LOST

chapter

APRIL 26, 1986.

For some it was just another ordinary day.

For others it was a day of shocking news.

But for us, it was the start of the new normal of living among the dead.

Awakened by a neighbor's early-morning phone call, our family entered into the living nightmare of the Chernobyl disaster. Toxic radioactive particles had blown in during the night from Ukraine. The rain sealed their deadly contamination into the soil and all of nature. We rushed to the balcony, hoping this was only a bad dream. The smell of death permeated the air. In a matter of hours, all living creatures, plants, and people suffered catastrophic effects.

---

[1] Miller, *Spirit, Work and Story*, 56–57.

What was green,
        was now brown.
                What was live,
                        was now dead.
A child conceived in a mother's womb was now
        abnormal,
                prematurely delivered, or
                      stillborn.

Human error had created the worst nuclear radiation accident in history.[2] Russia, Bulgaria, and most of Europe experienced the direct radioactive results, with devastating long-term effects on the whole planet as well. Predictions of the death toll going forward could not be quantified, though two decades later, statistics showed an estimated 270,000 who suffered from cancer and more than 100,000 who died within the first few years after the radiation.[3]

Fed only partial truths by the government-run media, we in Bulgaria were encouraged to go back to our normal lives. But there was no "normal." Death lay all around us, and we had little access to safe, uncontaminated liquids or food. Somehow, we were expected to remain calm and make sense out of burying the dead animals, boiling all the water, cutting fruits and vegetables to their core, and eating only those parts that didn't have dark spots of contamination.
        There were no other options.
                Survival was of the essence.
                Life had to be lived
                      amid these unknowns.

My parents and I drove immediately to my grandparents' village an hour away from our city, hoping to save some of our crops and livestock. Only a few sheep were still breathing; most of the chickens and other small animals had succumbed to the poison. Our well was contaminated, unusable, and the shallow river running through our land appeared dry. A gooey mud paste floated on top of the water. Mystified by the destruction all around and curious, I dipped my hand into the river. Instantly, my arm was covered with dark glop that burned my skin. I ran to the house and tried frantically to wash it off, but the substance was like stubborn glue. Several weeks passed before it was completely gone from my skin.

I watched my parents trudge down the narrow, muddy path through trees and

2 World Nuclear Association, "Health Impacts: Chernobyl Accident," www.world-nuclear.org.
3 Greenpeace International, "Chernobyl death toll grossly underestimated," www.greenpeace.org.

bushes that connected our home with the neighbors', carrying buckets of water back to the house from another well. Sprinting to meet them halfway, I saw the urgency in their eyes.

"Quickly! Help us get this water to the house," my dad insisted.

As I obeyed, my thoughts flashed to this same winding path I had trod so often as a little girl. Memories of my father carrying me on his shoulders when I got tired reminded me of how much I relied on his strength and my mother's comforting spirit. But now, we all needed to be there for each other and press through the despair for survival.

That day changed the meaning of the essence of life. Without notice, we had lost our bearings and now confronted the fearful fight against death itself. Sleeplessness and exhaustion didn't matter; the preservation of what was left of life was of greater importance. But safety was nowhere to be found as an entire community faced and dreaded the unknown. Who could possibly save us? There was no one!

> We were all affected.
> > We were all sick.
> > > We were all poisoned.
> > > > We were all alone.

But to submit to this tragedy was a choice, and we were not willing to become its victims. We embodied the fighter's spirit for survival.

> As long as a path was before us, we were
> > willing to stay on it.
> We were willing to learn a new level of endurance
> > for the sake of our families
> > > and for those who were fighting for life.
> As long as something was left in our hands, we still had a way out. Even if we held
> > one seed,
> > > one crop,
> > > > one gallon of water.
> > > > > It was enough to sustain hope.
> > > > > At least for a time.

THE DISGUISED STRANGER

When tragic events threaten our well-being, we go into survival mode. Unfortunately, an extended time in this way of life can carry long-term ramifications. Our focus turns inward, and the instinct for self-defense overrides our natural compassion and concern for others. The deep emotional perplexity depletes our energy and hardens our hearts.

Survival is driven by fear, and while fear may bring people to a temporary place of bonding, it can't provide long-term solutions and build resilience. Though individuals and communities came together to help each other after the radiation disaster, prolonged life under those circumstances, combined with the oppression and control of a strict dictatorship, began to breed a lifestyle of self-centeredness and manipulation based on survival. We soon found ourselves under a blanket of darkness, numb and hopeless.

If you had seen Bulgaria at that time—or any other nation, for that matter, where fear controls people—you would have noticed one predominant characteristic: a settled, gray nuance. The streets, buildings, statues, even the clothing, were primarily faded, natural tones devoid of energy and life. Fear drains the color from our lives, leaving only shades of gray that reveal the desperate cry of those trapped in fearful survival, longing for freedom.

You may never experience the consequences of radiation poisoning, but most likely you have dealt with fear, pain, and loss. Life proves to each of us that there will be moments
  of despair,
    terror,
      and utter aloneness.

No matter how many people may be walking alongside you, reliance upon them cannot be a substitute for peace and stability within. Their comforting words or empathetic acts of kindness can't ground you when your whole world is shaken and the pathway is dark. Yet something important takes place inside of you—your senses are awakened to the threat around you and your need for internal, mental, and emotional peace.
  Peace that derives from a greater source.
    Peace that surpasses all understanding.
      Peace that is necessary for the
        human soul to live at rest.

The question is, where do we find that peace?

We may see ourselves as the two disciples who walked the seven-mile dusty road to a village called Emmaus (Luke 24). I can only imagine the perplexity within their hearts. In search of answers and a reason to believe, perhaps they felt confusion, betrayal, fear, and uncertainty in the promises made to them by the Messiah. Could they believe the rumors that the One they loved had risen? Why hadn't He come to them? What did all this mean? The One they had followed,

the One who was to save them,

the One who was to give them eternal life,

was now gone,

crucified,

dead.

It must have seemed as if their world had crumbled around them. Sharing their sorrow with each other may have brought momentary comfort and emotional release from their pain but was not enough to sustain optimism for the future. The journey of life without the One they had believed in must have only seemed to seal the emptiness of their souls.

At that desperate moment He joined them.

Walking the path of their pain,

discussing the moments of their anguish,

listening to their questions.

Yet the story recounts that though Jesus walked with them, His identity was hidden from them. Their eyes saw only the stranger, not the resurrected Savior. "'Are you the only one visiting Jerusalem who does not know the things that have happened there in these days?'" asked one of them named Cleopas (Luke 24:18 NIV).

Perhaps their journey of silent discovery had greater importance than if Jesus had immediately satisfied their anxious questions. Disguised and unidentified, Christ often walks alongside us on the winding road filled with fear, questions, and sorrow. He is the only One who can carry us on His shoulders down the path, the way my father carried me. He is the only One who can quiet the burning within our hearts from the threats around us. And He is the One who opens our eyes to allow us to discover Him.

To seek Him in the darkest moments,

To ask Him back into our life's journey,

To meet the needs of the weary walking

alongside us.

At times in my travels, I have been joined by close friends, and I can attest to the comfort and strength they bring by their presence and conversation. But other times after long days of travel, we would be so physically or mentally exhausted that we had intervals of complete silence. Silence often scares people. We want to quickly replace the awkward feeling with a question or remark, even if it makes no sense. Yet these very moments of silence reveal the content or discontent in our hearts and the depth at which we are willing to listen—inwardly and outwardly. We may express a need or question aloud, but often the answers only come when there is enough silence for our souls to discern the solution.

In the silence of the journey we seek to understand.
　　In the silence of the journey we seek to create
　　　　the possible answers to unresolved questions,
　　　　　　the real solutions to existing problems.

And it is in the silence of that journey where we will eventually see our need for salvation, which has been provided by someone greater than us. A Savior, disguised as a man.
　　One of us, and yet without sin.
　　　　Not exempt from earthly temptations,
　　　　　　yet unyielding to their pull.
　　　　　　　　Above reproach, and yet human,
　　　　　　　　　　able to identify with our pain.
　　Whose immortality redeems us!
　　　　Whose love liberates us to live beyond the human coexistence
　　　　　　of dysfunctional reliance on one another,
　　　　　　　　leading us to eternal dependence on His sustaining power.

In many ways, the road to Emmaus reveals the yearning of our hearts for the search and reconnection to God from the separation experienced in the Garden of Eden.[4] In his book *Community 101,* French theologian Gilbert Bilezikian describes humanity's cry as

> *...the distant echo of the wail in the garden at the loss of innocence, of the grieving after a remembrance of shared freedom, of the release of body and soul to the embrace of absolute oneness. Our mourning is for the closeness that was ours by right of creation. Our grief is for the gift lost in the turmoil of rebellion. And now, whenever there is hope, our hope is for paradise regained, for human destiny remade in the redemptive restoration of community, the only certainty of oneness for here and for eternity.[5]*

In order for us to fully understand why Christ came, we must first know what we lost. Because Adam and Eve were created in God's image, they were made equal to each other, with unique abilities and individual responsibilities to populate the earth—to create a community that would express God's endless love for us. The disruption

---

[4] See Genesis 3 – The fall and separation of humanity from God's original plan.
[5] Bilezikian, *Community 101,* 15–16.

within this perfect creation happened after their decision to believe the voice of the serpent. They believed the serpent's lie that they were not made perfect and that God was withholding truth from them, which in turn led to separation between humanity and God, and to a broken-down society.

But God provided a way for redemption of our severed relationship with Him. Jesus came in order to restore God's original plan—oneness expressed in community and equality with one another. The Message Bible expresses Christ's dwelling among us in a beautiful way (John 1:14):

The Word became flesh and blood,
and moved into the neighborhood.
We saw the glory with our own eyes,
the one-of-a-kind glory,
like Father, like Son,
Generous inside and out,
true from start to finish.

Jesus continues to walk among us in the path of our human destruction until we recognize Him once again. Just as He asked Adam and Eve, "'Who told you that you were naked?'" (Genesis 3:11 MSG), He is asking us right now, "Who misled you? Who is filling your life and your future with fear?"

Fear creates noise.

Noise creates confusion.

Confusion creates unrest.

Unrest creates despair.

Despair causes darkness.

And darkness leads to blindness.

Often unable to recognize the One who has been walking with us all along, we look for an escape. The weary journey becomes our invisible mentor, but we usually cannot recognize it until we have reached the next destination. In order for our inner strength to develop, we must embrace this new mentor as we learn to recognize God's presence and experience His peace even amidst fearful and deadly circumstances.

When the two disciples arrived in Emmaus and sat down to eat with Jesus, they suddenly recognized Him for who He was—the risen Lord. His presence in the communion of their fellowship created an atmosphere of safety, which in turn opened their minds, hearts, and souls to feel joy and hope again. And in His presence, in communion with Him, your heartbeat is restored.

Once you are able to feel, you are also able to see.

Once you see Him,

you see restoration.

You see peace.

You see solutions.

You see redemption—

redemption through Christ that opens the doors to experience complete serenity and satisfaction.

The Brain, the Mind, and the Body

Based on God's vision for us to live in community and in a personal relationship with Him, we come to understand why healthy relational bonding is essential when we find ourselves in distressing situations. The calming effect that our mind desires is attachment through the presence of another. If no such person is present, the mind will regulate the flow of negative information through an increased flow of energy until emotional balance is achieved.

In the context of the brain and the body, "the mind is a process that regulates the flow of energy and information."[6] The brain is the social organ of the body. Attention, mood, thought, behavior, and every aspect of self-regulation depends on the integration taking place within the brain. Our experiences carry various emotions. When these positive or negative experiences are shared aloud in the presence of someone else, it allows these emotions to travel through and out of us, and the brain begins to remember them as a completed puzzle rather than as separate pieces.

In *The Whole-Brain Child*,[7] Dr. Siegel explains the functions of the brain through a hand illustration. A closed fist represents the whole brain. The "upstairs brain"—the cerebral cortex—is represented by the four fingers closed over the thumb. The upstairs brain directs our thoughts, meaning, logic, associations, and feelings. In spite of how often we think we are making choices and decisions with our logic center, only 20 percent of our decisions are made from the upstairs brain. The thumb represents the amygdala—our middle brain, which is the limbic system responsible for our emotions, survival instincts, and memory.

The wrist connection to our arm is our brain stem—the "downstairs brain." The downstairs brain connects our body, senses, appetite, autonomic functions, and

---

[6] Siegel, "Mindsight: The New Science," YouTube Video.
[7] Siegel and Bryson, *The Whole-Brain Child*, 37–63.

flight-flight responses to information from the upstairs brain. Because the brain stem is responsible for survival, 80 percent of our decisions are actually made from the downstairs brain.

Our body is the mechanism of the "know how" in the network between our brain and mind. After the fall of creation, our personal self-image experienced distortion and separation. Instead of living in interconnectivity of spirit, soul, and body— as a complete "me"— our "self" was divided. This led to equating self with our body image, without proper relation to the other two components that are part of self. Looking only on the outward appearance leads to unhealthy competition, jealousy, bitterness, and many other displays of the fallen state of humankind.

When threat occurs, we make immediate decisions to search for safety. The upstairs brain flips up, as represented by an open hand with four fingers raised. Our thumb remains closed, showing that the amygdala acts as a gate-reducing communication from the upstairs and downstairs brain. Dr. Siegel refers to this as a "flipping your lid" state of mind. When we assess the threat to be greater than our ability to create comfort and find protection, then anger, depression, frustration, anxiety, and emotional flashbacks are byproducts of our instinct to reach for a quick safety zone.

Since the fall of creation, humanity has been operating in a "flipped lid" state of mind.
What we should have enjoyed, we resented.
What we should have embraced, we rejected.
What we should have created, we destroyed.

We exchanged God's vision of us for a lie from the enemy.
We embraced distortion and called it a way of life.
We lost our perfect attachment to His security and
accepted regression to slavery.

From that moment on, our natural mind began looking for ways to channel our perceptions and construct our responses to the world. But nothing and no one can satisfy the longing for internal peace. Only the One who created the original picture can put together the puzzle of humanity's experiences, memories, and emotions in a new redeemed painting sealed by His love. Speaking through a prophet or sending an angel could never be enough. Love had to come in person and live among us as a human being.

Holding us gently.
Walking alongside us.
Empathizing with our pain.

Only then could we experience true connectedness and compassion for ourselves and others. Only then could we embrace a new life of restoration made possible through the provision of the cross. Our brain comes to a place of calm and our mind to a place of self-reflection, causing our bodies to experience tranquility and interconnectedness. That conscious quietness sets a specific sequence of neural processes in motion. Without thought and words, your mind is freed from its usual awareness of reality and self. This mental process generates an emotional discharge that you experience as awe. Awe of your Creator and assurance of the transformation to wholeness during your journey with Him.

REPOSITIONING THROUGH CONTEMPLATIVE PRAYER

My personal journey with Christ has led me on many winding roads. On some occasions, the narrow path was not wide enough for anyone else to travel with me. Walking with Him and learning to hear His voice built my confidence to trust Him utterly, releasing to Him the fear and anxiety in my heart.

In fact, the most solidifying times in my life have been the moments when I had no one else to talk to, especially while living in a foreign country. When we experience such aloneness, it is best not to try to fill the void with anything but communication with God. I learned early on, especially upon my arrival in the States, that unless I centered myself around Christ through prayer and meditation, the core of my being would be easily distressed.

During the summer break of 1995, shortly after I arrived in the States, my invisible mentor was the loneliness I felt each day—I had no one to talk to except God. Almost all the students had gone home to be with their families and the two students left were working full time. Every day I spoke to Jesus out loud, as though I could see Him present in my room. After two weeks of this daily practice, I began to feel His presence and hear His voice on a completely new level. My prayer no longer consisted of continuous rumbling; rather, it became more focused, with long intervals of meditating on a Scripture, a word, or an attribute of Christ's character. By the end of the summer, my mind was automatically processing my emotions, while my spirit was alive and connected with Jesus through the Holy Spirit. Fear of the unknown had been completely replaced with the presence of Christ.

The times when I have felt the most alive, energized, filled with peace and assurance have been generated through my conscious decision to quiet my mind and be still. This is called centering prayer or contemplative prayer where, according to neuroscientist Dr. Michael Spezio, there is "a suspension of all [narrative] and evaluative thought." This practice is an "intentional orientation in the mind to consent to the presence and connection of the Divine to all life at all times."[8]

The "consent" he mentions is simply to be aware of and acknowledge this connection. When we are unable—or unwilling—to recognize God's presence in our lives, it creates a void that leads to fear. Fear lowers our resilience to persevere during challenging circumstances and creates internal stress, which causes toxicity to be released in our cells. Some may not believe that we can live in a place where we no longer battle doubt or fear. Yet it is absolutely possible and even essential in order for us to live a healthy lifestyle.

Studies have shown that people who practice contemplative prayer develop a thicker and healthier frontal cortex of the brain. Prayer unifies the frontal cortex functions with the amygdala, sending messages of trust and healthy attachment to the middle brain. This strengthens the brain's social connectivity outside of prayer because it strengthens the middle prefrontal cortex. Stress, depression, and anxiety are decreased, because the interconnectivity of the brain, mind, and body is increased during prayer.

Dr. Spezio describes a comparative study done with three groups: one who utilized positive thinking, another who used relaxation techniques, and a third who used contemplative prayer. The group who used prayer as a lifestyle showed twice as much resilience amidst adversities and demonstrated greater strength and endurance, as well as an ability to remain at peace.[9]

One of the ways you can experience this type of grounding in your life is by meditating on a passage of Scripture for a full day, perhaps even a few days. Allow the words to settle in your mind and ask the Holy Spirit to give you a revelation and show you the connection of these words to your current journey. As we learned in previous chapters, we have a reticular activating system (RAS) that is constantly focusing our attention on that which is of value or threat to us. By consciously meditating on God's words, you begin to change the construct of your subconscious experiences as

---

[8] Spezio, "Mindfulness in the Brain," YouTube Video.
[9] Ibid.

you increase the value you put on who God is and decrease the threat from external, unknown circumstances.

Through the Valley of the Shadow of Death

"If you have God, you have everything"[10] becomes a revelation to us the moment we willingly accept the journey within the unknown. We embrace our invisible mentors of loneliness and survival by purposefully connecting our spirit, soul, and body with Christ. We walk with the inner assurance that the unfamiliar pathway through life has already been traveled by the One who loved us and chose us before He made this world.[11] It is on this life journey that we experience God as our Savior and also as our Shepherd. He not only rescues us during our greatest times of vulnerability but also comes to comfort, refresh, and satisfy our souls.

Trustful sheep with their loving shepherd.

Playing with the chickens while my dad tends the sheep.

While growing up, I often played with our sheep by tricking them to follow me outside their designated area, which caused them to get in trouble with my father. Just a few pieces of grass seemed enough to gain their trust. But it was not so on the day of the Chernobyl radiation. What appealed to them before no longer satisfied their urgent need for safety and comfort. As I watched them desperately trying to breathe, my presence only increased their anxiety. They knew I could not ease their pain because I had not shepherded them in the past. But as they heard my father's steps approach, a miracle transpired.

Their voices quieted.

Their bodies relaxed.

Their eyes closed.

---

[10] Ceitci Demirkova, *If You Have God, You Have Everything,* Gospel Media Sweden.

[11] "Even before He made the world, God loved us and chose us in Christ to be holy and without fault in his eyes" (Eph. 1:4 nlt).

The sense of his presence among them brought the peace they so desired. He was their true shepherd and they recognized him

by his smell,

his steps,

his presence.

Our soul recognizes its true Shepherd through the satisfaction only He can bring to our lives. When we experience His presence, our problems and worries begin to fade away. Our yearning to be refreshed and fully alive is completely satisfied only when we stop and become still. The glitzy social activities of life, like the small bunches of grass I used to tease the sheep, only create greater soul cravings within us. The words of Psalm 23:1–3 describe the ultimate revelation of His comfort we seek while walking the winding road: "The LORD is my shepherd; I shall not want. He makes me to lie down in green pastures; He leads me beside the still waters. He restores my soul."

I often observed our sheep's inability to rest at the appropriate times. During the sunny part of the day, their priority was eating; however, when a cloud formation blocked the sun, they would lie down and sleep. Unfortunately, the dark clouds indicated an upcoming storm and it was time for us to quickly move them back to safety. Too often, like the sheep, we lie down when challenges loom around us like dark clouds. Could it be we have confused the times to rest with the times to persevere? Accepted their momentary darkness as a permanent obstacle that foreshadows defeat? We must purposefully listen to the voice of our Shepherd to avoid these traps.

My own "shadow of death" experience came at age thirty-two when I received a disturbing phone call. The news I received reminded me that no matter how far I had come in life, the Chernobyl radiation was following me on my path like a dark cloud.

"We have found a thyroid imbalance, two tumors, and a cyst attached to your thyroid near your vocal cords. Please come back to the hospital for more tests." The straight path suddenly caved in before me, creating a valley where my knees buckled and my heart pounded. The radiation had affected my entire body, causing these frightening abnormalities.

Giving my mind a few minutes to catch up with the news, I paused. This was a crossroad—a choice had to be made. How did I want to face this road ahead? Consumed with fear or filled with peace? I intentionally chose the latter, and in that instant, peace flooded my being. God's presence covered me with a blanket of strength necessary for the new route of this journey. No matter how dark the valley that loomed ahead, my grounding in Him became my daily focus.

I created a small paper banner and called it "My Victory Banner." On one side I wrote Scripture verses that had become my life promises from God; on the other, I described how I saw myself walking on this new pathway. I included specific words: victorious, confident, mindful, strong, peaceful, fearless, whole, undeterred. Every day I held myself accountable to what I wrote, rather than what I felt, and was very deliberate in what I watched on TV or what I heard around me.

I embarked on a two-year restoration process through a naturopathic approach. My daily journey consisted of going through detoxification from the radiation and other toxins in my body. An alkaline diet and specific supplements strengthened my immune system and the proper function of my thyroid. Over time, my extreme fatigue, weight loss, hair loss, irregular heartbeats, and night sweats began to lessen. During the moments when my brain was stuck in a fog state from the detox, instead of focusing on the "what if's," I chose to write God's healing promises on 3 x 5 cards and place them on the bathroom mirror. Each morning I would read them out loud and envision the area of my neck healed—how it felt and looked without the tumors and cyst.

Once the pH levels in my body became alkaline balanced, the tumors began to dissolve. However, my system did not recognize the cyst as a foreign object, and the cyst did not respond to the change of my diet or to any supplemental intake. Instead of shrinking, it continued to grow, causing constant pressure on my vocal cords. One afternoon, as I was lying in my bed tired of the protruding cyst and of being sick, I began to pray with renewed confidence. New strength rose up in my spirit. I had assurance in my heart that I was being healed. At that moment I didn't feel anything. But when I woke the next morning and looked in the mirror, the cyst had disappeared. I could no longer see it or feel it. My nutritionist later confirmed that I had been healed and my body was free from the toxic radiation.

"Though I walk through the valley of the shadow of death, I will fear no evil, for You are with me; Your rod and Your staff, they comfort me" (Psalm 23:4). While healing may take place instantly at times, it can be a gradual process in other situations. It's important to remind ourselves that God is on the pathway with us and no matter what comes our way, He will give us the confidence and power to overcome, and the endurance to persevere while death may surround us.

> Our character is developed,
> our strength is built,
> our determination is wrapped in
> resilience when we choose
> to walk with Him.

Though the valley of the shadow of death may seem endless at times, don't stop
> believing,
>> moving,
>>> speaking.
Even if it's one verse of Scripture,
> one step,
>> one word,
stay focused on the One who creates a way in the midst of the impossible.

For the valleys of life reveal our invisible mentors. They open our eyes to see God's power as His shepherd's rod protecting us. And it is in our weakest moments when His staff uplifts our spirit into His presence of safety, security, and satisfaction. Even among the company of our enemies, our "cup will run over" (v. 5). Our true Shepherd severs the ties of our slavery to fear and reestablishes courage in us through the friendship we have in Him.

As shepherds in ancient times prepared the fields for the sheep, they would inspect the land for snakes. They poured a particular scented oil into the holes in the ground where the creatures would be hiding. The scent caused the snake to come out of its "cave," and in that instant, the shepherd would kill it with his rod. In addition, shepherds applied scented oil to the foreheads of the sheep, which protected them from being bitten by the snakes. The anointing God releases upon us as we walk the narrow, winding road with Him seals the victory of His redemption. We belong to Him, now and for eternity.

When you recognize Christ journeying alongside you,
> the road of survival becomes your road of revelation.
>> The road of despair becomes your road of
>>> empowerment.
>>>> The road of loneliness
>>>>> becomes your road of
>>>>>> peace, healing, and protection.

The longer you walk, the more you see.
> The more you see, the more you hunger.
>> The more you hunger, the more you
>>> choose to dwell in His house of refuge.
Where the haunting voice of fear is silenced;
>> Where His mercy and grace follow you
>>> all the days of your life.

AN EXPERIENTIAL IMAGERY EXERCISE

You may color it and write specific, positive words on the pathway that identify how you want to see yourself act, think, or respond while walking through the valleys of life.

PRINCIPLE

Internal peace is achieved when the spirit, soul, and body are interconnected. Contemplative prayer out of a personal relationship with Christ strengthens the frontal cortex of the brain and establishes greater inner resilience to persevere despite impossibilities. Fear is no longer a part of our journey when we recognize Christ's presence alongside us on the winding road through life.

Recall the moments when you know Jesus has carried you through the dark valleys.

-
-
-
-
-

-
-
-
-
-

In what way did you experience His presence during those times? Let that image sink in and create a visual picture of His unchanging love for you!

Write down 10 affirming victory words that will strengthen your faith and give you hope when all seems lost. Feel free to add Scripture verses next to them.

-
-
-
-
-
-
-
-
-

PATHWAY TO JOY

RISING STRONG FROM THE ASHES

chapter

Find a place **inside** where there's joy, and the joy will burn out the pain."[1]

– JOSEPH CAMPBELL

THE FLASHING lights and blaring sirens of a police car were fast approaching my vehicle. An innocent, ordinary evening of meetings had turned into quite an ordeal by 11 p.m.

Frightened.

    Shocked.

        Distressed.

My heart raced and my panic escalated. I looked in the rearview mirror, hoping for a miracle rescue as my car chugged to a stop in the middle of Interstate 5 in downtown Seattle. I had never been so relieved to hear the voice of a police officer as he shouted through the loudspeaker.

---

[1] Campbell and Osbon, *Reflections on The Art of Living,* Electronic Edition.

"Roll down your windows! Put your car in neutral! I will get you off the interstate safely."

Leaving the sirens wailing, the officer used the front bumper of his squad car to push my vehicle, slowly guiding it across six lanes of one-way traffic. My peace was restored as he continued to assure me of my safety through the loudspeaker. We pulled into a nearby gas station and in an instant, the officer appeared next to my car. He waved for me to get out of the vehicle as he opened the hood. Smoke mixed with the smell of rubber streamed from the engine.

"Looks like the front right wheel is about to detach from the axle. Also, your serpentine belt has snapped and your engine got overheated. You're lucky—this could have been much worse," he assessed. "We need to get you towed home."

Oh, no! Not again! I thought. It would be my second tow of the day. In the rush to be on time to my afternoon meetings, I had failed to see that the second floor of the parking ramp was designated one-hour parking only. A dark, empty parking spot awaited me when I returned four hours later. In frantic distress after a three-hour search for the correct impound lot, I finally reclaimed my car and paid the fine, only to find myself in this new predicament moments later.

Riding home in the tow truck at 1 a.m., I realized that the first towing must have caused all the new problems with the car. I had a 7 a.m. flight to catch for a speaking engagement, and I knew the importance of utilizing every minute of the night. So, I chose to let go of the frustration that had built up inside me and to deal with the car problems after my trip. But the night was not over yet.

In my apartment, still wearing my dress clothes from the meeting, I had just completed packing my suitcase when I heard a piercing, high-pitched beeping sound, escalating in intensity and volume.
Doors slamming.
     People running.
          Voices screaming.

The apartment below mine was on fire.

I grabbed my laptop and suitcase and joined the rest of the crowd as we rushed down five flights of stairs to safety.

The fire department and police arrived within minutes. For the next three hours we watched in awe as they quenched the fire and kept the rest of the building from going up in flames. A few of the firefighters came to the area where the frightened residents were standing. With a calm voice, one of them explained what to expect once we reentered the building, and which stairway to use. The smell of smoke was still fresh in the air, and many of the units had water damage from the automated sprinklers. It was a dismal scene that suggested months of repairs and renovation ahead.

I turned my attention to the firefighter helping me carry my luggage up the stairs. "Are you ever afraid to go into a flaming building?" I asked.

"Not at all. I am never afraid," he replied. "This is what gives me thrill and excitement. I'm ready to jump into the flames. We're well trained to operate under these circumstances."

His words, spoken with such
    certainty,
        confidence,
            security, and
                boldness,
painted a strong picture of reassurance and trust—someone who does not fear but instead leaps into danger to save others at the risk of his own life.

Quickly checking my condo for water damage, I was relieved to see that none of the sprinklers had activated. Before I could catch my breath, I heard a honk echo in the quiet street below. The taxi taking me to the airport had arrived. I snatched up my belongings and dashed back down the stairs.

"How is your morning going?" the driver's friendly voice greeted me.

I took a deep breath. I was about to burst as countless
emotions,
    images,
        and unbelievable stories,
            replayed in my mind.

"It's great," I said with a polite smile, hoping to prevent further questions. But as my thoughts turned from the panic of the past hours to God's hand on each situation, I realized it was true—I was thankful to be alive and grateful for His protection and love every step of the way.

THE QUEST FOR COMEBACK

Perhaps you have had similar experiences to mine, days with the most unexpected endings. Thankfully, my challenges were short term, though it felt like a decade of living packed into one day.

But sometimes life can lead us in another direction—a difficult season that catches us unaware with its harsh reality and unwelcome circumstances. Traumatic events leave us reeling. The place of safety where you once parked your dreams is now a distant echo of what life used to be before your soul was towed into this unwanted season.

Your vision is replaced with blindness.
Your laughter is silenced through rejection.
Your joy is flooded with mourning.
Your light is swallowed by fire.
Your life is buried in a pile of ashes.

And sometimes, in an effort to cope, we overstay our time here rather than travel through, parking in the long-term lot instead of the visitor's spot. Emotions like resentment, anger, bitterness, and hopelessness hold us captive and before we know it, we feel
displaced,
disconnected,
damaged,
discouraged.

We have lost our joy.

How do we find our way home? How can we reconnect to ourselves, God, and others to find joy and wholeness?

In the New Testament, one Jewish family found themselves in a similar quandary of questions and fears. John 11:1–44 brings us into their shaken reality. The story reveals the heartbreak of two sisters, Mary and Martha, who counted on Christ's timely return to heal their brother Lazarus. "'Master, the one you love so very much is sick'" (v. 3 MSG) was their anguished cry.

His quick reply, "'This sickness is not unto death'" (v. 4) eased everyone's worries at first. But intentionally postponing His return to Bethany by two days, Jesus appeared on the scene after Lazarus had been dead for four days. "'Master, if only you had been here, my brother would not have died'" (v. 32 MSG), Martha told him. Both sisters were overwhelmed by sorrow and grief, unhappy with His absence during their tragedy.

The passage unveils insightful revelation. As we learned in Chapter 7, during a season of distress, we crave safe bonding with someone who knows our true core. In order for our minds to remain at peace, we search for a person who will empathize with our hurt and be present with us on the journey. Further, during times of sorrow, we are also looking to regain our joy amidst the pain through an attachment we perceive would be safe for us.

Scientifically viewed, our brain is not wired for sadness. We were created to live and experience continuous joy through our relationship with one another, while abiding in God's presence. Only in Him is the "fullness of joy" (Psalm 16:11) continuously present. The moment we are disconnected from joy through negative experiences, we tend to run away.

Away from pain.

Away from emptiness.

Away from God.

Unfortunately, the farther we run from God, the closer we run to anger, blame, distress, and despair.

When Jesus went to Lazarus' house, He found Mary and Martha in a similar frame of mind.

Sad.

Confused.

Hurt.

As their souls flooded with sorrow, they began to detach from Him emotionally. It seemed like Lazarus was not the only one dead. His family and friends who had wrapped him in grave clothes and laid him in the dark cave had partly died with him that day as well. Their grief and hopelessness caused them to question Christ's promises and disconnect their trust in Him.

Why did Jesus wait to resurrect Lazarus until the fourth day? I believe His intentional delay was for two reasons. According to Jewish belief at the time, it was possible for someone to come back to life on or prior to the third day of death. However, they did not believe that a resurrection could occur on the fourth day.[2] Jesus showed that not only did He have power to raise the dead, but on an even greater level of importance, He joined them in their sorrow to reconnect them to Himself.

The story records the most profound release of empathy at the loss experienced by Mary, Martha, and the others present. "Jesus wept" (v. 35) is the shortest verse in the

---

[2] For additional insight on these Scriptures and Jewish tradition, see Israel Institute of Biblical Studies, "Resurrection of Lazarus, Jews and Jewish Tradition," Dr. Eli Lizorkin-Eyzenberg.

Bible, expressing the deepest emotion of a God fully present and fully human amidst our pain. With His tears, Jesus validated their loss; and with His words and actions, He safely moved them from a place of mourning into a place of joy.

Discovering Your "Joy Camp"

The feeling of being understood and comforted during distress or celebrated when reaching an achievement, especially during childhood development, causes us to create a secure attachment with those around us. Healthy bonding times between parent and child are vital in establishing a safe attachment pattern necessary for our well-being as adults. People with secure attachment styles typically have greater confidence and satisfaction in life and in relationships.[3]

When healthy support and bonding don't happen, unhealthy attachment styles can develop, resulting in adults who cling too closely to a partner for safety, or those who distance themselves emotionally and detach from loved ones, or some who fear both being too close or too distant from others.[4] As adults, we begin to rely on our unconsciously developed behaviors from childhood to later fill the need for acceptance, satisfaction, and joy.

Psychologist and theologian Dr. James Wilder explains how secure or safe attachments help us create a proper view of our external circumstances and build healthy wiring of our nervous system in response to joy through bonding. Until that state of mind is achieved, he explains, people are always in a place of searching for joy in life through either positive or negative attachment and detachment behaviors.

Dr. Wilder describes our path to joy with a camping analogy. In camping, the first activity is to set up base camp, a home to return to after our wilderness adventures. In the same way, our nervous system seeks to return to its natural state of joy —our "joy camp."[5] It's where we live, our natural destination.

He emphasizes that our nervous system is designed to "rest in a state of joy, not in a state of upset."[6] Being upset leads to increased stress levels within the body, which cause anxiety, panic, and fear to steal the centrality of our joy. Joy is distinct from happiness because it is internal and part of the wiring of our brain. Happiness, on the other hand, is external, lived in short intervals, and carries no sustainability to empower us from within.

---

3 Firestone, "How Your Attachment Style Impacts Your Relationship," PsychologyToday.com.
4 Ibid.
5 Wilder, "Developing Joy Strength," YouTube Video.
6 Ibid.

If Jesus had healed Lazarus before he died, instant happiness would have come to the entire family and community; however, it would have been based on a quick external experience without internal revelation of joy. By walking the pathway of sorrow after Lazarus' death onto the pathway to joy after his resurrection, their faith was reconnected with Christ's character, rather than with faith in His miracles.

They cried together.

They laughed together,

They rejoiced together.

They shared together.

These experiences prepared them to face the future with greater inner strength and enduring hope.

Our personal stories evoke great emotional connection that helps us form a bond with those around us. When you share your story, you build empathy as well as stimulate ideas, thoughts, and emotions in the listener's brain. The same applies when you hear friends relate their experiences. Without knowing, remembering, and sharing our stories, we would have no connection to one another. The basic joy factor the nervous system seeks is for someone we perceive as safe to be with us as we journey through life. Talking, laughing, crying, singing, and showing affection are all variations of bonding with one another.

However, they are limited connections to joy and are dependent on the ability of each person to be fully himself or herself. If we don't know how to be ourselves

in times of sorrow,

in times of threat,

in times of loss, even in

times of victory,

our emotions, thoughts, and feelings will not be freely expressed.

Often we hide the dark gaps of our absent personality and lost hope behind the walls of addictions and detachment from people and reality. We crave

closeness,

safety, and

intimacy,

but the moment we come near them, the fear of losing the connection exceeds the present joy and we quickly push others away. "This is too good to be true. I wonder how long this will last?" we ask ourselves, afraid to fully feel.

REBUILDING YOUR PATHWAY TO JOY

In addition to contemplative prayer discussed in the previous chapter, the process of journeying from safety through sorrow and back to safety through safe attachment, rebuilds what Dr. Wilder calls our "joy mountain."[7] It expands the ability of the frontal cortex of our mind to stay resilient under excruciating circumstances. The longer someone remains with you through a sorrowful time, the less fearful you become of pain. Through that connection, you develop a pathway of safe return to joy. Like a compass, it guides you to your core friends and liberates you to stay true to yourself at all times.

Your quest to be fully alive leads you to discover at least three types of people along the pathway of life. Those who journey with you when all is well remain seasonal friends. They will change often, depending on the circumstances and their level of endurance. Others will come along and guide you off the interstate when your engine fails, or fearlessly enter a burning building to help you escape. They are transitional friends but important to embrace as mentors. You need their wisdom, confidence, and assistance when you can no longer continue forward.

Then on occasion, you will meet a few people—perhaps only a handful—willing to stay on the pathway with you. They become your core soul friends.
>   Without pretense.
>   · Calling you to the best version of your true self.
Their voices remind you to stay fully engaged,
>   fully present,
>   and fully aware
of your emotional, mental, and spiritual state during your personal quest of rediscovery.

After experiencing the blessing of friends, favor, and connections while living in Tulsa, I was offered an opportunity to work on evangelism outreaches with the team of a newly formed church in a Midwestern city. With hope and anticipation, I relocated. But the moment I crossed the Missouri state line, I felt a shifting. For the next three years, I embarked on the journey of rediscovering and regaining my joy. Every day I felt stripped of my "coat of many colors," my earthly source of security and identity. Everything I held close was removed from me, and I found myself once again stranded at a different "interstate of life," but this time
>   without close friends,
>   without much money,
>   without a reliable car,
>   without a computer, and
>   without a permanent place to live.

---

[7] Ibid.

The more I tried to do everything right, the worse it became. One night during my journaling, I sensed God's presence. His voice gently spoke to my heart, "If you learn how to find daily joy while walking through this season of loss, you can live anywhere in the world and you will always be able make it."

New determination arose within me. The length of this season depended entirely on my willingness to adapt to these changes. I needed to remind myself who I was from the pages of the journals I kept over the years. I began to unwrap the "death clothes" trying to choke my life, as I chose to write and later publish my first book, *If You Have God, You Have Everything.* I had to do something tangible while adjusting my mind-set. Purposefully, I parked my car each week in a visitor's parking spot at various locations to remind myself, *I am only visiting this season of life.*

I can even recall the moment when I found the pathway to joy. I was reading Acts 26:2 where Paul was standing before King Agrippa making his case after being falsely accused by the Jews. "I think myself happy" was the start of his speech. Though various translations have different versions of this verse, I chose to adopt this one into my daily vocabulary. Accepting that season brought joy and laughter back into my life. I allowed myself to fully embrace the pain of the sorrow, without worrying that in my emptiness, I might not meet the expectations of others. Numerous times during the day, I forgave those who had hurt me. Forgiveness opened the doors for me to journey right into the lives of my new best friends, my next mentors, and my most compassionate lifelong partners.

During that season, I allowed myself to accept my humanity without trying to be perfect, and to find beauty among the ashes. And somehow, in a way that only God can fulfill the impossible, the puzzle pieces fell into place. During one of the darkest seasons of my life, I laughed more than I cried through the pain.

It is mystery.

It is paradox.

It is irony.

I found the pathway of joy through suffering while journeying back to wholeness of self.

Seasons are not a sprint.

Sorrow cannot be rushed.

Ashes are difficult to scoop up and throw away.

The faster you try to remove them, the more they float into the air. They reveal to everyone else the debris of your life. The only escape is to accept the difficulties of that season, be your true self, adapt to the changes, and pursue the path that leads you to joy mountain.

And one day you wake up and look in the mirror and finally ask some honest questions: *Who am I? What have I become? How much longer am I willing to dwell in this land?* That quest for a comeback begins to energize us. The breeze of life floods your inner being with the vibrant memories of past experiences, colored by fun and adventure. *Keep on remembering… Keep on answering the hard questions… Keep on searching…* For a brief moment you feel the heartbeat returning to your dreams. *But not so fast—there is more to learn,* the voice of your invisible mentor calls through the darkness of your cave. What more could you possibly be taught?

In the times when we feel like we have absolutely nothing to give, it's important to go back and remind ourselves of
the miracles,
     the victories,
          the stories,
               the laughter.

You must draw strength from the previous seasons of the familiar. From the times that brought you
     the greatest joy,
          the greatest revelation,
               the greatest achievement.

Let these memories carry you like waves into the next season of self-discovery. No, you are not going back, you are only drawing from the well of your greatest moments. It's a reminder that deep inside, the voice of your soul is awakening to see—beyond the dark, empty burial cave—the new you arising strong out of the ashes.

That's what I did at the time. I reminded myself of a moment during my college years when I had to let go of my last $2 tucked safely in my wallet. The money was not enough to pay my tuition or buy food, yet knowing that I still had something to hold on to brought comfort. That is, until the moment when I felt God's voice nudging my heart to buy a hamburger for someone else. *Really? With my last $2?* But how could I object? I had nothing to lose. I was at the bottom, and the only option was to give what was in my hand and expect by faith that God would meet my need. Something happens inside you when you have absolutely nothing to hold on to, not even a cent. God is your only source. This liberating experience creates a permanent pathway to joy and a voice of victory that no one can silence.

In a forest devastated by fire, life is emerging even among the ashes. Rejuvenation and re-creation are stimulated. Nature is designed to reproduce itself and return to a place of abundance and life through the seeds of plants. The jack pine tree, for example, sheds its seeds within a pinecone. However, the cone itself can remain sealed for years and will usually only open under extreme heat, 122°F (50°C) or greater.[8] This type of tree emerges out of disaster and grows while everything around it is dead.

Like the jack pine, you are a carrier of many seeds and have the ability to reproduce life even when disaster strikes. By releasing your seeds along the way, you create a pathway to your joy camp. Each time you plant, it becomes easier to remember how far you have come. The ashes dissipate underneath the new life. The small seed we hold in our hands can create stability and a miracle in our lives only when we release it.

The moment I let go, I opened the door to an incredible financial breakthrough. Without it, I would not be here today. Before noon the next day, upon arrival at my college, I was asked to go to the director's office. No matter what they would have said to me that day, I had made up my mind that somehow, some way, I would graduate. It was my testing time, to see if I would give myself a premature exit before arrival at my final destination. But a miracle transpired. The night before, the directors of my college and my program had decided that I should receive a scholarship and complete all my schooling without having to worry about monthly tuition. That day I received a full scholarship, fully paid housing, and money to buy food for the next few months till I was able to work.

Celebrating a personal victory—my 1997 graduation from Victory Bible College in Tulsa!

Pastor Billy Joe Daugherty and the happy graduate.

Over the years, I have kept a record of many of God's miracles because it's important to remember them, especially during tough seasons. It's necessary to cultivate those seeds inside of us and release them in times when the ashes are all we can see.

---

[8] "Jack Pine Cone Type," DNR.WI.gov.

And now,
     you discover
         the one who is
no longer frightened,
     no longer shocked,
         no longer distressed.
The one who is found.
     The one who is whole.
The one who has discovered the pathway
     back to joy.

AN EXPERIENTIAL IMAGERY EXERCISE

You may color it and write on each side of the pathway leading to "Joy Camp." Write dates, locations, or seasons, below or next to the signs, of the times you experienced joy or faced hardship. Try to place them chronologically so you will have a better visual.

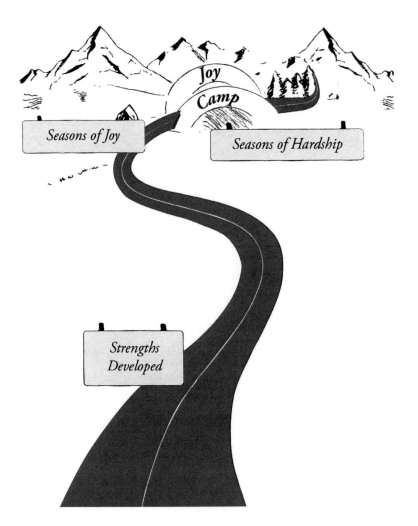

Suggestion: *Consider keeping a journal of times when you are especially aware of God's faithfulness in your life. Write down several Scripture verses that can bring encouragement to you in a difficult season. (For example, Isaiah 41:10: "'Fear not, for I am with you; be not dismayed, for I am your God. I will strengthen you, yes, I will help you, I will uphold you with My righteous right hand.'")*

PRINCIPLE

We are wired for joy, not sorrow. The fear of losing our safety and joy drives us toward the embrace of addictions, insecure attachment styles, and behaviors that numb our feelings. Story-sharing moments in the presence of a safe friend recreate connection and lead to healthy bonding. In order to find our way through the seasons of sorrow, covered in ashes, we must identify the seed we still possess and plant it in the ground before moving on to the next season.

Briefly recall some times in your life when you experienced adversity. *What miracles have sprung forth from the ashes of these times? Take time to recall joy that God has restored to your life after a loss. Choose to remember times that put a smile on your face.*

Take the time *to recreate your pathway to a place of safety and joy by writing down the following: Who are your core friends? List them and describe the qualities that you treasure in your friendship with each of them.*

Think of characteristics, beliefs, and strengths you developed during your times of hardship. Which ones could you utilize when empathizing with a friend who may be going through a hard time? How could your story encourage him or her and establish a safe connection?

Ask yourself if there are people in your past or present whom you need to forgive. Sometimes you may even need to forgive yourself. By utilizing the principles in this chapter, remind yourself that you are not a victim of your circumstances. You can remove "the grave clothes" by learning how to tell your story through the lens of victory as you embrace the truth that God has been and will always be present in your life.

What seeds could you plant along the pathway of ashes in order for new life and joy to reemerge inside of you?

A LIFE OF GREATNESS

POURED OUT AS LIQUID GOLD

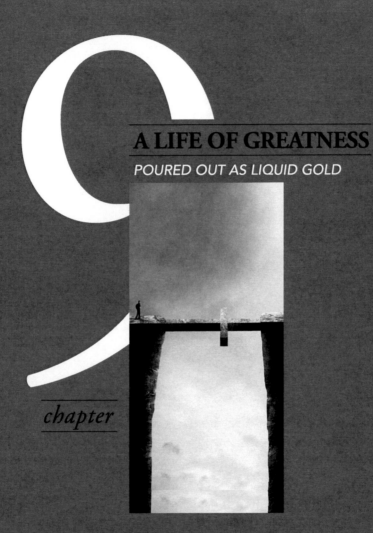

chapter

> "To live a life of courage is not a guarantee of prestige or adulation....It only matters if you live and die fulfilling the mission you were born for."[1]
>
> – ERWIN MCMANUS

BUILDING MY sand castle near the shore, I was so proud of my creativity. Not many families and children were at the beach, since it was late afternoon on a cloudy day. I didn't have to protect my amazing sand empire from being destroyed by the negligence of passersby. Fixated on the wonder of what I had made, I noticed a fast-approaching threat from the corner of my eye. I was so focused on avoiding the obvious danger—people who could damage my work—that I did not pay attention to how close I was to the incoming tide. Without permission, a giant wave splashed on the shore and furiously rushed over the compacted wet sand, approaching my fragile creation. Sweeping past the sand castle gates, the wave swallowed one of my scoops. I jumped up, fearless, to save my tools and ran after the water-thief. As a seven-year-old child, I didn't pay attention to the height of the waves.

---

[1] McManus, *Uprising*, 63.

Though they had scared me before, I was boldly going to show them who was in charge. Until they kept hitting me, knocking me down, one after another. It seemed like the entire ocean wanted to conquer me. Swallowing the salt water, I could no longer breathe.

I lost my balance.

I lost my stamina.

I lost my fight.

The only thing I could remember was someone picking me up just before I hit what seemed like the bottom of the Black Sea. He carried me quickly back to shore and laid me on the sand. My blurry vision cleared, and there was my rescuer, my hero—my father! He had saved me from drowning. My mom held me and comforted my aching body. I was so lucky to have parents like them. We didn't have much, but

My wonderful parents, Angel and Slavka.

we were never poor because we had each other. For years, I was traumatized by this unfortunate incident. Water, oceans, and waves were not something I could enjoy but resentfully feared—they had tried to take my life!

Perhaps at times in our earthly journey we have built sand castles—a grand empire for show that has become our obsession, our pride and joy, something by which to impress others. *Look at me—how clever I am and what an incredible life I have built.* We often become fixated on what we have, unable to see the dangers lurking around us. Or, we lose our judgment, blind to reason when something threatens our precious, precarious creation.

At other times our sand castle serves as a proud façade that looks good from the outside—we can hide behind it, protecting ourselves from the world of hurt and rejection by living in false humility. We barricade ourselves, wary of external intrusion that could take us down—like other passersby running on the beach. What we may not realize is that kingdoms have sometimes failed because of inside adversaries, not always outside intruders. The very waves that brought in the wet, heavy sand for me to build my kingdom were the ones that as easily washed it away.

Or, is it possible that we have become our own enemy? Running headlong into danger to protect our fragile world at any cost. Has our pride crumbled our accomplishments from within and become a wave destroying those closest to us? While our kingdom may crumble amidst treason, God's Kingdom

> consumes,
>> overtakes, and
>>> delivers

the shortcomings of our fragile humanity through His active love

> willing to forgive,
>> willing to suffer,
>>> willing to die.

Even while our kingdom is a proud display, adored from afar, God's Kingdom is

> fluid,
>> active, and
>>> living
>>>> within us.[2]

How quickly we forget who we are and in whose image we were created when we choose to build and place our treasure on the wrong soil. We proudly display the beauty of our small earthly kingdom, mistaking it for greatness. The truth is that we often diminish ourselves this way. We become hostages of our own achievements rather than owning them and making decisions out of our own free will. We avoid transparency by hiding, and we cover up our shortcomings with religious rituals. Like an ocean wave over our sand castle, our achievements wash back into the ground and out to sea, taking us with them.

Popularity easily becomes an obsession; money and prestige blind us from recognizing the difference between character traits and flashy talents. Perhaps even our faith in God becomes an ideology we exalt, rather than an active force of Christ's love permeating our lives. We become hollow because we have tried to escape difficulty rather than pressing through it with transparency, learning from it, and understanding how to love who we are and those entrusted to us. In the rush to prove to the world who we are becoming, we neglect to rewrite the negative emotional history stored in our subconscious mind. The more indebted we become to our earthly empires, the greater emptiness we feel inside.

How easy it is to create our sand castle so everyone else, perhaps even we, can admire it. Yet, how quickly

> one mistake,
>> one hardship,

---

[2] Luke 17:20–21.

one person,

one loss,

can wash it into the sea of unforgettable regret. No one wants to live life as a failure. We want to wake up each morning believing that what we try to achieve during our lifetime will have significance and meaning to the generations after us. We don't like to be wrong. But do we justify our rightness without willingness to expose our frailty?

In a world where people love to be admired and only pretend to love others, Jesus demonstrated a life without pretense. He came in humility with genuine love. He didn't come to prove His greatness; He came to heal our brokenness. It is hard to understand the upside-down paradigm of Christ the Servant, rather than Christ the King. Through His willing sacrifice on the cross, He lowered the gates of heaven to kiss the face of this earth.

Betrayal was swallowed through His death.

Redemption was sealed through His resurrection.

God's Kingdom has an open door policy established on a freewill principle. It reads, "Whoever believes in Him should not perish, but have everlasting life" (John 3:16). His sacrifice is for all humanity. His love invites us to come just as we are—with all of our fears, doubts, and mistakes. But He leaves the choice to believe in Him up to you and me.

Without coercion,

without manipulation,

without pretense.

Tzarevetz castle, Veliko Turnovo. The castle's gate lowers to form a bridge, just as Christ's sacrifice created a bridge for humanity.

Inviting God's Kingdom to abide inside of you does not demean your power to choose. As you welcome God to fill your life, you slowly let down your guard, your façades, and allow others in. Not because you are no longer afraid of being wounded, but because you are able to overcome your hurts through authentic relationship and ownership of your stories. The impossibilities no longer scare you. Now their whisper has become an invisible mentor, a guiding voice that unlocks your past and your present. Inviting them to fearlessly live together in your conscious awareness. This is the platform for the birth of innovative future:

Where your life becomes the substance to feed starving souls because you own both your mistakes and your successes.

Where your dreams and ambitions add seasoning to whet the appetite of
those still searching for true meaning and purpose.
Where you stand on the bridge between God and humanity,
offering His sustenance to them, your life an offering that
brings healing.

LIVING A LIFE OF GREATNESS AND THE CHARACTER TEST

I still remember the concerned look in my teacher's eyes as he handed me my graded essay. He shook his head. "How much longer will you be writing about this Jesus of yours?" he said. "Every essay for the past year is about Him. We are studying Bulgarian literature. You can no longer create your own theme and write about God, otherwise I will fail you from graduating."

His reasonable warning should have scared me, yet for the next two years of high school, I continued to write without altering my style. Out of compassion, he gave me a passing grade upon graduation, and as an expression of my gratitude, I brought him a gift. Unsure of what to expect, he slowly unwrapped the shiny paper to reveal a Bible. His eyes caught my name and phone number under an inscription I had written on the inside page: "This is the most important book you will ever read. I hope you take the time to do so. You would make a great Christian someday."

"Thank you, but I don't think I will have time to read this," he replied with a stern voice as he walked away.

Nearly eight years passed. Each time I went back to my hometown, I tried to find him. He seemed to have vanished; no one knew where he was or what had happened to him after our graduation. Until one day, in the spring of 2002, my cell phone rang. With overflowing enthusiasm, my mom told me of a call she had received earlier in the day. My teacher was still alive and he was looking for me! Heart racing and hands shaking, I dialed his number.

"My mom said you had called. You still remember me after all these years?" I quietly asked.

The moment he heard my voice, he began to cry. "How could I forget you!" he replied.

With words choked by tears, he began to paint a beautiful picture of God's redemption and love. Shortly after my graduation he had experienced a stroke. Left paralyzed with almost complete memory loss, he said only one person came to his mind. "Your name, your big blue eyes, and your voice telling me about Jesus is the only thing that I could recall. For years, the words in your essays were all I could remember."

During the next few years while he lay in bed, his wife read to him from that Bible every night. With each passing day he regained
> more of his strength,
>> more of his mobility, and
>>> more of his memory.

"Thank you for sharing Jesus with me and not giving up on me," he continued. "Today I can walk and talk again because of Him. But most importantly, He is not only your Savior, but now He is also mine. What you told me was the only truth I needed to know, and I am eternally grateful."

Hearing his story was both emotional and serene. It solidified in my heart a more profound understanding of God's personal grace and love for another human being. I can't help but wonder what would have happened to my teacher if I had not been bold enough to stand for what I believed. Would he have lived? Where would he have spent eternity? Would there have been a miraculous ending amidst such unpredictable circumstances? Remembering his last words to me over the phone stimulates my heart's passion to continually reject conformity, stay bold, and share God's truth regardless of others' opinions.

Conforming to the world—being average—does not bring healing to people who are bleeding from the wounds of their shattered lives. Accepting a life of mediocrity may shield you from a temporary rejection, but refusing to rise above it will haunt you forever. Step up to what you are called to do and create a transformational ripple effect in the world around you through your faith in God and your testimony.

> Follow the stirring.
>> Hear the rumble.
>>> Be the movement.

You and I are called to greatness, not a fleeting fame. We are called to
> stand up for truth,
>> stand for justice, and
>>> stand with Christ,

at the risk of living as outcasts.

We are called to greatness through passion that burns within us so strongly and so deeply that it liquefies our lives.

When we no longer care about the approval of others
>or the rejection from our enemies.
>>When our names are remembered not
>>>because of our achievements but because
>>>>of our willingness to embrace, without
>>>>>question, the sharp edges of others'
>>>>>>brokenness.

Even if we bleed.
>Even if we are humiliated.
>Even if we die.

In that moment, in our human suffering, we can truly identify with Christ and His journey on this earth. Abandoned by most of His followers who didn't agree with His words, Jesus brought disturbance and uprising among the masses, not popularity.

"'Therefore, I have said to you that no one can come to Me unless it has been granted to him by My Father'" (John 6:65). Jesus' zeal and love was expressed directly and loudly enough for everyone to hear, for everyone to make his or her own decision.

"'Do you also want to go away?'" He asked His twelve disciples (v. 67).

Without hesitation Peter replied, "'Lord, to whom shall we go? You have the words of eternal life'" (v. 68).

Peter could sense the life of greatness he and the disciples were offered. But at the time he gave an answer, his understanding of a life of commitment to Christ—even to the point of suffering—was only a conceptual belief, not a tested reality. Often we may find ourselves like Peter. Our words can sound impressive, even sincere, but without enough substance to back them up.

As one of the main outspoken risk-takers among the twelve,
>his loyalty was tried and
>>his commitment judged.
The first trial resulted in him betraying Christ on the night before the crucifixion. The second generated personal resentment and shame after the death of His Savior.

No matter how great Peter's intentions were and how notable his promises sounded, his natural abilities failed him—
>before the disciples,
>>before the observers,
>>>before Jesus.

The resurrection of Jesus on the third day changed everything—for the whole world and for each one of us. The door to eternal freedom and life was opened to humanity. Peter was given a second chance to emerge from a setback of humiliation and enter into a comeback to wholeness.

"'He is risen from the dead….Now go and tell His disciples, including Peter'" was the instruction of the angel to the women at the tomb (Mark 16: 6–7 NLT). These two powerful words, *including Peter*, caused shame to be lifted and forgiveness and confidence to flow back into the soul of this man. They washed away his anxiety and openly proclaimed before the world that

> Jesus still remembered him,
>> Jesus still trusted him,
>>> Jesus still loved him.

LIVING A LIFE OF GREATNESS—POURED OUT AS GOLD

In Japanese culture, a method called *kintsugi*[3] is used to repair broken pieces of ceramic with gold, silver, or platinum. When the liquefied state of these expensive metals is poured between the broken pieces of the containers, the brokenness no longer displays fragility. It now stands for beauty. The cracks are sealed permanently, adding new originality to the vessels, immediately making them more valuable than before.

Peter experienced his greatest restoration of human brokenness through the love of Christ being poured between the cracks of his frailty. He became the strongest while in his weakness. Peter's future was not pointless because of a mistake. It was enlarged because of Christ's perfect sacrifice. God's love flowed like a golden stream through the broken parts of Peter's heart, restoring

> his value,
>> his dignity, and
>>> his calling.

At the beginning of his discipleship, Peter's life was like a hardened gold—beautiful and expensive, beckoning admiration, and even arousing jealousy in others. But no matter how impressive Peter appeared on the outside, he was not yet able to feed the generations to come. Until the day he lost his grip. His image as a prestigious fishermen and a faithful disciple of Christ was shattered in three consecutive instances through his words of denial: "I don't know this man" (see Luke 22:54–62). The day Peter felt his own despair became the day he consciously faced his invisible mentor of denial and betrayal.

---

[3] Jobson, "Kintsugi," www.thisiscolossal.com.

This time, however, no matter
> how much he knew,
>> how strong he felt,
>>> how great his calling,

what started unintentionally out of boastfulness was about to destroy him inwardly and utterly.

The best way to stop an unintentional fire is to draw an intentional fire line near the destruction. A backfire is set on this control line and burns everything consumable, so when the encroaching fire arrives, it has no fuel to keep going and dies out. God, as our all-consuming fire,[4] stepped deliberately
> into the field of Peter's condemnation,
>> onto the land of our sin,
>>> before the fire of human self-destruction.

In order for Peter's denial to be redeemed, both his pride and shame had to be consumed through the intentional fire line Jesus offered him.

Shortly after His resurrection, Jesus met with Peter on the shore of the Sea of Galilee. There He reinstated Peter's calling by asking him three separate times, "'Simon, son of Jonah, do you love Me?'" (John 21:15–17). With each affirmative answer Peter gave, he chose to step
> into a deeper understanding of Christ's forgiveness,
>> into a broader knowledge of Christ's love,
>>> into a greater purification through Christ's fire.

Peter arose to greatness in his life as an apostle because the external fire of his self-righteousness no longer consumed him. His redemption was expressed
> through his passion,
>> his convictions,
>>> his life,

motivated by the internal fire deposited in him the day Jesus entrusted him to go and feed His sheep (v. 17). Finally Peter had something to offer to the world—the true heart of Jesus.

History is made up of many tiers of kingdoms, empires, and people who came before us.
> Some conquered through power.
>> Some lived for power.
>>> Some fought against power.

---

[4] Hebrews 12:29.

Often, we must dig through layers of the past to discover fundamental truths. I find European history fascinating as I read about the conquests and the losses. The areas of what is today Southern Bulgaria, Macedonia, Greece, and Turkey, were years ago the lands where the Apostle Paul and the early Church lived and traveled. If you continue to journey to the west, you will run into the Basilica of San Clemente in Vatican City, Rome, constructed upon three layers of history stacked on top of one another.[5]

Where the Roman and the Egyptian empires ruled.
Where the crypts of the first-century Church saints lie.
Where Peter was crucified upside down,
counting himself unworthy of the
same death as His Savior.

Today, people from around the world come to the modern Saint Peter's Basilica built directly above his tomb.[6] In an incongruous way, they step above the blood and sacrifice of Peter and others like him, whose lives had become liquefied through fire in order to be "poured out as a drink offering" into the lives of others (Phil 2:17).

Even the Hollywood Walk of Fame, which boasts more than 2,500 terrazzo and brass stars embedded in the sidewalks of Los Angeles honoring celebrities and cultural icons, becomes just another sidewalk on a rainy day. No matter how admired and respected these famous names may be, their individual greatness becomes almost unrecognizable under the drops of rain. The real question for us is, are we willing to remain nameless stars whose identity may never be listed on any Walk of Fame? Are we willing to be a part of history, where our ceiling becomes the platform for someone else to step upon?

As God pours His healing love into the cracks of our broken lives, our vessel becomes a beautiful reflection of His artistry. "We have this treasure in earthen vessels, that the excellency of the power may be of God, and not of us" (2 Cor. 4:7). Then we in turn can be used as liquid gold in the lives of others, as His love is poured out through us to bring healing and restoration.

When gold is in a liquid state, it doesn't lose its value or its strength. However,
it can no longer be captured,
it can no longer be held, and
it can no longer be placed on a pedestal.

A supernatural miracle transpires at the moment the liquid love of God is poured

---

[5] For more information, read: basilicasanclemente.com.
[6] "Saint Peter's Basilica," New World Encyclopedia, www.newworldencyclopedia.org.

across our hearts (Romans 5:5). A new spark is ignited within our dim lives.

His power,

His authority,

His light,

hidden under the layers of our human core, empower us by sealing the cracks of our brokenness with a golden thread. The most astounding fact is that we, who are like fragile clay jars, have been entrusted to contain this great treasure.

Just like Peter, we are continually offered second chances. And with these second chances come the opportunity to answer the final question Jesus asked Peter. Do we love Him enough to lose our lives in order to find them? Do we love Him enough to become nameless cornerstones within the human foundation? Do we love Him enough to, in turn, flow as liquid gold to seal the cracks of humanity's shortcomings?

Then our lives experience greatness, which is

strong enough to solidify our value because of

our faith in God;

pure enough to create acceptance

through safe bonding;

transparent enough to show the world

freedom through forgiveness.

FINDING OUR TRUE HOME

People from around the world gathered at Christ Chapel on the campus of Oral Roberts University in Tulsa on March 6, 2013, to pay tribute to the life of Dr. T.L. Osborn. He pioneered world-changing evangelism marked by astounding miracles, proclaiming the Gospel to millions of people in more than 100 countries.[7] For over half a century, Dr. T.L., his wife Dr. Daisy, and their daughter Dr. LaDonna Osborn set a precedent for true evangelism. My personal relationship with them through the years has enriched my life and caused me to rise to a greater level of

character,

strength, and

excellence.

A statement I heard that day made a lasting impression in my life. "When other people came to our nation to preach the Gospel, we knew all about them and their accomplishments. When the Osborn family came to preach, we knew nothing about

---

[7] For more information about Osborn Ministries International, visit www.osborn.org.

them, but we heard about who we could be and what we could become. They didn't give us themselves. They gave us Jesus!"

Our greatest impact on this earth
       is not validated through mere accomplishments,
           but through great humility.
      Is not quantified through successful achievements,
           but through deep trust.
      Is not exemplified through self-seeking glorification,
           but through selfless servitude.

One day, all of our names will lie hidden underneath the layers of history's debris. What will matter is not how successful we were in protecting our sand castles, but rather how much of Jesus' love was poured out of our hearts. Because His love is liquid, it heals,
      it flows,
          it connects,
              it binds,
                  it builds.

It creates the life we all want to have, experience, and live. No longer frightened by what we could become. Rather, becoming the reflection of the One in whom we have believed.
      Now we stand boldly.
          Now we stand complete.
              Now we stand found by Him.
Prepared to live.
      Willing to give.
          Unashamed to say,
Where else could we go Lord? You alone have the words that give eternal life.

THAT'S OUR HOME!

AN EXPERIENTIAL IMAGERY EXERCISE

You may color it inside the vase or around the cracks, and write down areas that you would like to seal in someone's life (or in the world) as if you were liquefied gold. How could the world be a better place because of your contribution?

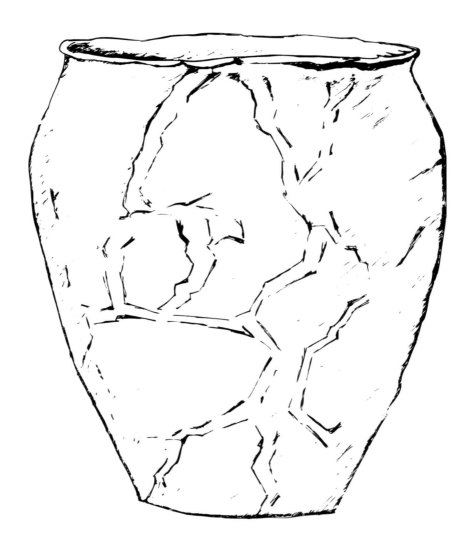

PRINCIPLE

We are compelled to love and show compassion to all people because of Christ who has loved us first and has become our Savior. Our lives become liquefied gold when God's fire ignites our passion and when His sacrifice on the cross seals our redemption. We cannot be contained. We are called to live a life of greatness.

Take the time *to remember when you fully surrendered each area of your life to Christ, when you allowed Him to fill your life with love and compassion for someone else. What did you do? Write specific examples.*

In which areas of your life would you like to become more generous, loving, and compassionate?

List 5–10 talents (gifts) that you would like to utilize to enrich someone's life:

-
-
-
-
-
-
-
-
-
-

Your talents, gifts, and vision are valuable and they are needed in the world today. What kind of difference would you like to make (for a person, family, nation/s) that you believe would portray a life of significance?

RISING ABOVE THE IMPOSSIBLE

WRITING YOUR STORY OF INVISIBLE MENTORS

chapter

Showing up is our power.

Story is our way home.

Truth is our song.

We are the brave and brokenhearted.

We are rising strong."[1]

– BRENÉ BROWN

CONGRATULATIONS, Brave Sojourner! You did it!

We have journeyed together through the pages of this book, learning how to recognize our invisible mentors in the impossible circumstances of life. We found a life in which…

⌐●   we can fearlessly ***dance on hot coals***, no matter the size of the crowd or the opinions of others. The fire purifies our motives, exposes our weaknesses, and causes us to live authentically, so that we can help rescue those who are consumed by the flames of fear and hopelessness. That is our life's passion!

---

[1] Brown, *Rising Strong*, 267.

⅃•   *surviving on the bus ride of life* no longer threatens us but gives us the inner strength and perseverance to face the journey with greater confidence. As we learn to trust God and His rich promises, we move from shame to authenticity. That's our self-discovery!

⅃•   we climb the *152 stairs to contentment,* empowered and unashamed to run through the desert of our past and use the stairs of our memories as a bridge to our future. Our memories are no longer orphaned but live unapologetically in our present. That's our freedom!

⅃•   our *dreams take flight.* We kiss them goodnight through our imagination and envision ourselves within them. We give them purpose so they can develop and become an inspiration for others to dream bigger than themselves. That's our opportunity!

⅃•   we *skydive with a 12,000-foot perspective* onto the landing of our destiny, welcoming our gliding process to rest in the Lord, mirror His character, and prepare for our next assignment. That's our strength!

⅃•   we are *liberated from our invisible crutches* when we identify our fears. We overcome impossibilities, turning them into invisible mentors by leaving our empty vessels at the well with Jesus, so we can live a shame-free life. That's our empowerment!

⅃•   we *find restoration when all seems lost* and new resilience through contemplative prayer. We join the Good Shepherd on the winding road through the valleys of life, no longer afraid of fear itself. Our internal peace is once again reestablished through the proper integration of our spirit, soul, and body. That's our assimilation!

⅃•   we travel the *pathway to joy*, rising strong from the ashes of our life. We learn the importance of sharing our story with a safe friend, and seed our pathway to authenticity and victory. That's our emerging!

⅃•   we are poured like *liquid gold* into the cracks of humanity to create strength and restore value—compelled to show compassion to all people because Christ sealed the cracks in our lives with His liquid love and redemption. That's our motivation!

We identified
    the faces of our invisible mentors.
        We incorporated
            the process of their mentorship.
            We embraced
                the motivation
                    to rise from…
                    to rise within…
                    to rise above…
                every impossibility we encounter.

Now I pass the baton into your hands, commissioning you to live and love others and yourself with brave authenticity.
    Explore far.
        Travel wide.
            Remain present.

Remember your home is Jesus. Always stay close to Him!
    He is the initiator of our stories,
        the comma in our transitions,
            the period in our boundaries,
                the exclamation point in our lives!

In the final pages of this book, I encourage you to take the opportunity to write the beautiful beginning of your story through this journey's discoveries.
    No one can write it better than you.
        No one can own it more than you.
            No one can feel it more deeply than you.

Your story is birthed not out of motivation
    to challenge,
        to overcome, or
            to explain the impossible.
Your story is birthed from within the depths of your heart as a testament to the world of who you are because of embracing your invisible mentors and accepting the impossible as an internal stepping-stone that leads you to greater bravery, defined strength, and eternal truth.

The impossible is your life—Recognize it!
    The impossible is your assignment—Accept it!
        The impossible is your destiny—Live it!

AN EXPERIENTIAL IMAGERY EXERCISE

You may color it and write inside the pathway some of the areas you would like to explore—actual destinations such as cities or countries, or individual goals for spiritual, mental, and physical development.

PRINCIPLE

God is the author of our stories. Always remember to come home to Him.

Write your story, *based upon the principles you have learned and the revelations and discoveries you have made while reading this book. Let your heart speak! It has a voice that wants to be heard. Even if you write only a few sentences or paragraphs, take the time to do so. This is just the beginning of greater depth and freedom in your life.*

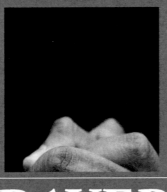

PRAYERS

PRAYER OF SALVATION

If this book has touched your heart and you desire to make Christ your personal Lord and Savior, the prayer below will assist you in entering into a personal relationship—not with a religion or rituals, but with God, who loves you unconditionally.

You may read this (example) prayer out loud or create your own in similar wording. What matters is not how well you read it or say it but the sincerity of your heart.

Dear Lord Jesus,
I acknowledge you as the only true God, through whom I can obtain salvation and receive forgiveness. I repent of my sins, and I ask for your forgiveness and freedom. I give you full access to my heart and my life. Fill me with your Holy Spirit, and guide me each day. I ask for your help, wisdom, and strength. I choose to follow you and serve you from this day forward to eternity. In the Name of Jesus, Amen!

PRAYER OF RESTORATION AND REDEDICATION

If you already believe in God, but your heart has grown cold toward Him over the years, today you have an opportunity to come back to Him. He wants to restore your life and heal your broken heart.

You may read this (example) prayer out loud or create your own in similar wording. Be sincere and honest—God hears you and loves you! He has never left you and will never abandon you!

Dear Lord Jesus,
Today I choose to return to you—my true home. I no longer desire to wander through life alone. Restore the years I have spent away from you. Remove the hardness in me and heal my hurting heart. I want to fall in love with you once again, as I did on that day when I first asked you into my heart. I place my life in your hands and ask for your guidance and assistance. I desire to serve you for the rest of my life! In Jesus' Name, Amen!

PRAYER FOR DELIVERANCE FROM OPPRESSION OR DEPRESSION

Oppression or depression can influence us at various seasons in life, especially when faced with trials and challenges. We need God's help to overcome and be liberated from the bondage of depression.

You may read this (example) prayer out loud or create your own in similar wording. God is present in your trials and He is willing to help you, heal you, and love you through it all.

Dear Lord Jesus,
I need your help in overcoming this _____ (depression, addiction, oppression—you name the problem). I ask that your power would destroy that yoke of bondage in my life and I would be completely set free in my mind and emotions. I speak soundness in my mind and wholeness to my body. I choose to think and believe what you say about me in your Word, and not the voices of impossibilities in my life. In your Name, I command the spirits of depression and oppression to leave my life; they are no longer a part of me. Thank you for setting me free, that I may be a testimony for your glory! In Jesus' Name, Amen!

BIBLIOGRAPHY

Babbel, Susanne. "Post Traumatic Stress Disorder After 9/11 and Katrina." *Psychology Today.* Accessed February 6, 2017. https://www.psychologytoday.com/blog/somatic-psychology/201109/post-traumatic-stress-disorder-after-911-and-katrina.

"Basilica." http://basilicasanclemente.com/eng/index.php/history/basilica.

Bilezikian, Gilbert G. *Community 101: Reclaiming The Church as Community of Oneness.* Grand Rapids, MI: Zondervan Pub. House, 1997: 15–16.

Bonanno, George A., Sandro Galea, Angela Bucciarelli, and David Vlahov. "What predicts psychological resilience after disaster? The role of demographics, resources, and life stress." *Journal of Consulting and Clinical Psychology* 75, no. 5 (2007): 671-82. doi:10.1037/0022-006x.75.5.671.

BookLover (Author). "The Treasury of Motivational Quotes - Kindle Edition." Self-Help Kindle eBooks @ Amazon.com. January 20, 2016. https://www.amazon.com/dp/B01BCLOTZC.

Brown, Brené. "Are You Judging Those Who Ask for Help?" Oprah's Life Class, Oprah Winfrey Network. YouTube. September 22, 2013. http://youtu.be/Iud89Gi8Jgs.

Brown, Brené. *Daring Greatly: How the courage to be vulnerable transforms the way we live, love, parent, and lead.* New York, NY: Gotham Books, 2012: 33.

Brown, Brené. *Rising Strong: The reckoning. The rumble. The revolution.* New York: Spiegel & Grau, 2015: 267.

Campbell, Joseph, and Diane K. Osbon. *A Joseph Campbell Companion: Reflections on The Art of Living.* Electronic Edition. San Anselmo, CA: Joseph Campbell Foundation, 2011.

"Commemoration of Vassil Levski." The Info List. http://www.theinfolist.com/php/SummaryGet.php?FindGo=Commemoration%20Of%20Vassil%20Levski.

Cooper, Robert K. *The Other 90%: How to unlock your vast untapped potential for leadership and life.* New York: Crown Business, 2001: 21–22.

Demirkova, Ceitci. *If You Have God You Have Everything: A faith adventure of a young Bulgarian woman.* Hällefors: Gospel Media Sweden, 2002.

Dobrev, Dobri. "Elder Dobri from Baylovo – Bulgaria," YouTube, July 13, 2009, https://www.youtube.com/watch?v=vaau8iT0D0o.; originally from the film *Mite,* 26:31, produced in 2000 by the Pokrov Foundation. 1:22-1:25.

Firestone, Lisa. "How Your Attachment Style Impacts Your Relationship." *Psychology Today.* July 30, 2013. Accessed February 6, 2017. https://www.psychologytoday.com/blog/compassion-matters/201307/how-your-attachment-style-impacts-your-relationship.

Frankl, Viktor E. *Man's Search for Meaning: An introduction to logotherapy.* Boston: Beacon Press, 1992: 117.

Greenpeace International. "Chernobyl death toll grossly underestimated." April 18, 2006. http://www.greenpeace.org/international/en/news/features/chernobyl-deaths-180406/.

Heberle, Manuela. "Three Stages Of Memory in Psychology: Explanation & Summary." Study.com, accessed February 6, 2017. http://study.com/academy/lesson/three-stages-of-memory-in-psychology-explanation-lesson-quiz.html.

Holy Bible: New Living Translation. Wheaton, IL: Tyndale House Publishers, 1996.

"Jack Pine Cone Type, Chapter 33." Forest Management. http://dnr.wi.gov/topic/ForestManagement/documents/24315/33.pdf.

Jobson, Christopher. "Kintsugi: The Art of Broken Pieces." *Colossal.* May 8, 2014. Accessed February 6, 2017. http://www.thisiscolossal.com/2014/05/kintsugi-the-art-of-broken-pieces/.

Konnikova, Maria. "How People Learn to Become Resilient." *The New Yorker.* February 11, 2016. http://www.newyorker.com/science/maria-konnikova/the-secret-formula-for-resilience.

"Lecture Demonstration Manual." Lecture Demonstration Manual. UCLA Physics & Astronomy. http://www.physics.ucla.edu/demoweb/dod/firewalking.html.

Lewis, C. S. *The Complete C.S. Lewis Signature Classics.* New York, NY: HarperOne, 2002: 168.

The Living Bible. Tyndale House Publishers, 1971.

"Living Bulwark." Living Bulwark. http://www.swordofthespirit.net/bulwark/truehumilitychart.htm.

Lizorkin-Eyzenberg, Eli. "Resurrection of Lazarus, Jews and Jewish Tradition (John 11:1–44)." November 28, 2013, accessed March 10, 2017. http://jewishstudies. eteacherbiblical.com/resurrection-lazarus-jewish-tradition-john-121-44/.

Longfellow, Henry Wadsworth. "The Ladder of St. Augustine." Henry Wadsworth Longfellow, Maine Historical Society, http://www.hwlongfellow.org.

McManus, Erwin Raphael. *Uprising: A revolution of the soul.* Nashville: T. Nelson, 2003: 63.

McManus, Erwin Raphael. *The Artisan Soul: Crafting your life into a work of art.* San Francisco: HarperOne, 2014: 100.

McManus, Erwin Raphael. *Stand Against The Wind: Awaken the hero within.* Nashville: J. Countryman, 2006: 81–82.

Miller, Calvin. *Spirit, Work, and Story* (Grand Rapids, Baker, 1996): 56–57.

National Transportation Safety Board. "NTSB releases final report on investigation of crash of aircraft piloted by John F. Kennedy Jr." July 6, 2000. https://app.ntsb.gov/news/200/000706.htm.

Neria, Yuval, Laura DiGrande, and Ben G. Adams. "Posttraumatic Stress Disorder Following the September 11, 2001, Terrorist Attacks: A Review of the Literature Among Highly Exposed Populations." *The American Psychologist.* September 2011. https://www.ncbi.nlm.nih.gov/pmc/articles/PMC3386850/. In a longitudinal survey representative of adults living in NYC one and two years after 9/11, it was found that the prevalence of PTSD declined from 5% at 12 months after 9/11 to 3.8% at 24 months after 9/11 (rates at both time points were based on the 71% of the baseline sample that was retained at follow-up; Adams & Boscarino, 2006). Also, at 24 months post-attack, 3.9% of this sample was identified as having delayed PTSD.

Neuburger, Mary. "R. J. Crampton. Bulgaria. (Oxford History of Modern Europe.) New York: Oxford University Press. 2007. xxi, 507." *The American Historical Review 113*, no. 1 (2008): 89–90. doi:10.1086/ahr.113.1.283.

The Pacific Institute (R) LLC. *Thought Patterns for High Performance 3.0* (R). Seattle, WA: Pacific Institute Publishing, 2009.

Patel, Ushma. "Hurricane Katrina survivors struggle with mental health years later, study says." Princeton University. January 24, 2012. http://www.princeton.edu/main/news/archive/S32/74/14C15/index.xml?section=topstories. "About 33 percent of the participants still had PTSS, and 30 percent had psychological distress. Though levels for both conditions had declined from the first follow-up 11 months after the hurricane, they were not back to pre-hurricane levels."

Pearce, T. M. "The English Proverb in New Mexico." *California Folklore Quarterly* 5, no. 4 (1946): 354. doi:10.2307/1495928.

Peterson, Eugene H. *The Message.* Colorado Springs, CO: NavPress, 2004.

Plutarch. BrainyQuote.com, Xplore Inc, https://www.brainyquote.com/quotes/quotes/p/plutarch120365.html.

ReaganFoundation. "'Berlin Wall' Speech – President Reagan's Address at the Brandenburg Gate – 6/12/87." YouTube. April 15, 2009. https://www.youtube.com/watch?v=5MDFX-dNtsM. 11:16–12:03; 24:34–25:22.

"Saint Peter." Saint Peter – New World Encyclopedia. Accessed February 6, 2017. http://www.newworldencyclopedia.org/entry/St._Peter's_Basilica.

Siegel, Daniel J. "Google Personal Growth Series: Mindsight: The New Science of," YouTube. April 23, 2009: 5:21–7:48. Combined definition from a teaching by Dr. Daniel Siegel. GoogleTechTalks with Daniel Siegel. https://www.youtube.com/watch?v=Gr4Od7kqDT8&feature=youtube.

Siegel, Daniel J., and Tina Payne Bryson. *The Whole-Brain Child: 12 proven strategies to nurture your child's developing mind.* New York: Bantam Books Trade Paperbacks, 2012: 37–63, 99, 103, 124–125.

Sinek, Simon. TEDtalksDirector. "How great leaders inspire action." YouTube, May 4, 2010. https://www.youtube.com/watch?v=qp0HIF3SfI4. 15:21–17:15.

Spezio, Michael. "Mindfulness in the Brain." YouTube. October 15, 2009. https://www.youtube.com/watch?v=bmmd2cqjdsU.

Spirit-Filled Life Bible. Nashville: Thomas Nelson Publishers, 1991.

Spitzer Center Blog. "Presentation on Creation Draws Large Crowd." http://www.spitzercenter.org/html/faith-side/about-us/spitzer-blog.php.

Spitzer Center. "The Four Levels Defined,"accessed February 6, 2017. http://www.spitzercenter.org/html/archive/our-approach/the-four-levels-defined.php.

"Strong's Hebrew: 6960. (qavah) – wait." Accessed February 6, 2017. http://biblehub.com/hebrew/6960.htm.

Ten Boom, Corrie. *The Hiding Place.* 35th ed. Grand Rapids, MI: Chosen Books, a division of Baker Publishing Group, 2011, 150.

Tice, Louis E., and Joyce Quick. *Personal Coaching for Results: How to mentor and inspire others to amazing growth.* Nashville: Thomas Nelson Publishers, a division of Thomas Nelson, Inc., 1997, 94–96.

Van Der Kolk, "Keynote Session: Complex Trauma: Developmental & Neurobiological Impact with Dr. Bessel van der Kolk," MercyHomeBG. YouTube. October 28, 2016, https://www.youtube.com/watch?v=gXr_IB1ELCk.

Van Gogh, Vincent. Ronald de Leeuw (Editor), Arnold J. Pomerans (Translator). "Vincent Van Gogh." Goodreads. https://www.goodreads.com/author/quotes/34583.Vincent_Van_Gogh.

Waters, Everett, David Corcoran, and Meltem Anafarta. "Attachment, Other Relationships, and the Theory that All Good Things Go Together." *Human Development* 48, no. 1-2 (2005): 80-84. doi:10.1159/000083217.

Wickstrom, Steven P. "Wait upon the Lord." http://www.spwickstrom.com/wait/.

Wilder, James. "Developing Joy Strength." Deeperwalk. YouTube. March 18, 2014. https://www.youtube.com/watch?v=8ghOKPRWrao. 1:06:02–1:14:13.

World Nuclear Association. "Health Impacts: Chernobyl Accident," Chernobyl Accident: Health Impacts. December 2014, accessed February 5, 2017. http://www.world-nuclear.org/information-library/safety-and-security/safety-of-plants/appendices/chernobyl-accident-appendix-2-health-impacts.aspx.

Yontef, Gary. "Awareness, Dialogue, and Process, *Gestalt Therapy:* An Introduction." Gestalt Therapy: An Introduction, 1993, accessed January 5, 2017. http://www.gestalt.org/yontef.

ABOUT THE AUTHOR

Born and raised in Bulgaria, a former communist country, Ceitci's story is one of tragedy to triumph and poverty to riches. Arriving in the United States at age nineteen with $100 and 100 words of English, her ultimate passion and purpose was, and still is, helping people. Her personal stories of overcoming life's challenges and persevering in the face of betrayal, discouragement, and sickness are intertwined with her principles of hope, truth, love, and purpose.

After extensive studies in cross-cultural communications, public speaking, business and leadership development, Ceitci has become a recognized motivational speaker and teacher worldwide. As an ordained minister, she specializes in a wide range of topics pertaining to Christian theology, nonprofit organizational growth, creative fundraising methods, as well as personal and spiritual development of our God-given potential and gifts. She has been a guest on Clear Channel networks, numerous TV and radio shows, and has spoken to a variety of audiences, churches, and business organizations.

As the Founder and CEO of the nonprofit organization Ceitci Demirkova Ministries/Changing a Generation, formed in 1995, Ceitci and her team work in Bulgaria, Ghana, and Uganda. The organization assists with the social empowerment of orphans, children, and youth through business development, education, and partnerships with organizations similar in vision and purpose.

Ceitci is a former project director and a certified facilitator with five of the programs of The Pacific Institute in Seattle, Washington. In addition, she is certified with PeopleBest, Inc., in Orange County, California, as a DNA Assessment Trainer, Level 1.

In addition to the book *Motivated by the Impossible,* Ceitci has authored an autobiography, *If You Have God, You Have Everything,* and the three-volume devotional series *A Cup of Inspiration.*

BOOK ORDERS

To order additional copies of this book and Ceitci's other titles, please contact:

Ceitci Demirkova Ministries
Tel.: 206-569-5161
E-mail: info@ceitci.org
Web: www.ceitci.org
Web: www.invisiblementors.com

The book is also available for purchase on Amazon.com and CreateSpace.com in both Kindle and paperback.

For interviews, bookings, or to sponsor a child, contact:

**Ceitci Demirkova Ministries /
Changing a Generation**
206-569-5161
info@ceitci.org
www.ceitci.org
www.changingageneration.net
www.invisiblementors.com

Follow us on social media:

Facebook
www.facebook.com/MotivatedByTheImpossible
www.facebook.com/ChangingAGeneration
Twitter
twitter.com/ceitci
twitter.com/CG_1LifeATaTime
twitter.com/PurposeRevealed
Instagram
www.instagram.com/invisiblementors
YouTube
www.youtube.com/user/CeitciDemirkova